TECHNICAL PRACTICES TO MAXIMISE PERFORMANCE

50 TECHNICAL PRACTICES | YOUTH TO PRO | TRAINING WEEK | FOOTBALL PERIODIZATION

Written by
ADAM OWEN PhD

UEFA Pro Coaching Licence

Published by

TECHNICAL PRACTICES TO MAXIMISE PERFORMANCE

50 TECHNICAL PRACTICES | YOUTH TO PRO | TRAINING WEEK | FOOTBALL PERIODIZATION

First published November 2024 by SoccerTutor.com
info@soccertutor.com | www.SoccerTutor.com

UK: 0208 1234 007 | **US:** (305) 767 4443 | **ROTW:** +44 208 1234 007
ISBN: 978-1-910491-70-6

Copyright: SoccerTutor.com Limited © 2024. All Rights Reserved.

All rights reserved. No part of this publication may be reproduced, stored in a retrieval system, or transmitted in any form or by any means, electronic, mechanical, photocopy, recording or otherwise, without prior written permission of the copyright owner. Nor can it be circulated in any form of binding or cover other than that in which it is published and without similar condition including this condition being imposed on a subsequent purchaser.

Written by Adam Owen

Edited by Alex Fitzgerald - SoccerTutor.com

Diagrams

Diagram designs by SoccerTutor.com. All the diagrams in this book have been created using SoccerTutor.com Tactics Manager Software available from www.SoccerTutor.com

Note: While every effort has been made to ensure the technical accuracy of the content of this book, neither the author nor publishers can accept any responsibility for any injury or loss sustained as a result of the use of this material.

CONTENTS

Dr. Adam Owen: Coach Profile 6
Dr. Adam Owen: Career of High Performance Expert 8
How this Book Fits into the "Football Periodization to Maximise Performance" Philosophy 9
Benefits of Technical Practices to Maximise Training Outcomes 10
Technical Development in Football Periodization Methodology 11
Diagram Key 12
Practice Format 12

The Training Week 13

Practice Design Considerations to Optimise Coaching Outcomes 14
Training Session Flow 15
Practical Coaching Model to Build the Training Week (Microcycle) 17
Periodization, Tapering Strategy and Maximising Performance 18
The Training Week: Professional Microcycle 19
Training Session Format for Professional Microcycle 20
The Training Week: Semi-Professional Microcycle 21
The Training Week: Youth Academy Microcycle 22
The Training Week: Grassroots (Youth) Microcycle 1 23
The Training Week: Grassroots (Youth) Microcycle 2 24
Analysis of a 6-Week Training Mesocycle and Positional Quantification in Elite European Football Players 25

Periodization of Technical Training 26

Periodization of Technical Practices in Football Training 27
Intensive and Extensive Technical Practices 28
Intensive and Extensive Technical Passing Actions in Football 29
Considerations of the Microcycle (Training Week) 30

Passing Analysis: Highlighting the Technical Requirements of Elite Players 31

Technical Passing Performance of Elite Midfielder Rodri (Ballon d'Or Winner) 32
Technical Passing in Football: Lessons from Rodri's Elite Performance 35
Passing Dominance in La Liga: Real Madrid and Barcelona 36
Analysis of Passing and Goal Scoring Trends at International Tournaments 37

Breaking Lines and Passing Distances 38
Tactical Insights and Practical Applications for Coaches 40
Further Technical Research Findings in Elite Professional Football 41
Impact of Player Movements When Receiving Passes (La Liga Study) 42
Summary of the La Liga Study Findings 43

Intensive Technical Practices (Small Spaces) 44

Intensive Technical Actions and Practices in Small Spaces 45
Intensive Technical Practices within the Training Week (Microcycle) 46
Intensive Technical Training Session - 4 Days Until Match (MD +3/-4) Example ... 47
Intensive Technical Training Session - 2 Days Until Match (MD +5/-2) Example ... 48
MD +3/-4 and MD +5/-2 - Intensive Technical Practices 49
Key Coaching Points for Intensive Technical Practices (Small Spaces) 50
1. Juventus Dynamic Speed and Agility Movements Technical Circuit 51
2. Real Madrid "In and Out" Dribbling and Passing Circuit 52
3. Technical Receiving (Body Shape) Rotational Passing Combinations 53
4. Bayern Munich Open Up to Receive Play Through and Around Passing .. 54
5. Technical Receiving and Support Play Passing Combinations 55
6. Up, Back, and Through Passing and Switching Play Combination 56
7. End to End Third Man Run Combinations to Play Forward 57
8. Ajax Triangle Open Up to Receive Rotational Passing 58
9. Ajax Triangle Rotational Passing with One-Two Support Play 59
10. Ajax Triangle One-Two Support and Quick Combination Play 60
11. Ajax Triangle Free Player Decision Making Passing Combinations 61
12. Aerial Passing and Receiving Technical Triangle 62
13. High Speed Triangle Combination Play with Angled Passing 63
14. Up, Back, and Through with Give & Go Speed and Timing Passing "Y" . 64
15. Up, Back, Through, and Around Passing "Y" with Angled Forward Passing ... 65
16. Passing Combination Play and Dribbling Technical Skills "Y" Passing Race ... 66
17. Create Space to Lose a Defender and Scanning Double Movement Diamond Passing ... 67
18. Pass and Make Opposite Movement "Cross Shape" Diamond Passing .. 68
19. Play Wide and Through Diamond Passing Combinations 69
20. High Speed One Touch Diamond Support Play Passing Combinations .. 70
21. Inter Milan Passing, Receiving, and Quick Combination Play 71
22. FC Barcelona Small Spaces "Figure of 8" Progressing Play Combinations ... 72
23. FC Barcelona One-Touch Passing Combinations to Play Forward 73
24. Individual Technical Skills: Receiving, Passing, Turning, and Dribbling ... 74
25. Ladder High Speed Passing, Back Foot Receiving, and Shooting 75

26. Manchester City One-Touch Passing and Finishing Target Goal Race 76

Extensive Technical Practices (Large Spaces) 77

Extensive Technical Actions and Practices 78
Extensive Technical Practices within the Training Week (Microcycle) 79
Extensive Technical Training Session - 3 Days Until Match (MD +4/-3) Example 80
MD +4/-3 - Extensive Technical Practices 81
Key Coaching Points for Extensive Technical Practices (Large Spaces) 82
1. Receiving Under Pressure and Dribbling Skills Passing "Y" 83
2. Changing Lines and Angles Passing Combinations and Support Play 84
3. PSG Switching Play Passing and Receiving Rotations 85
4. Technical Rotational Passing Race (Progressive Pattern) 86
5. FC Barcelona "Figure of 8" Progressing Play Combinations and Support Play 87
6. FC Barcelona "Figure of 8" Progressing Play Combinations and Support Play (Progression) 88
7. Ajax One-Twos, Movement, Timing, and Positional Passing 89
8. Rotational Passing Combinations with Overlap Third Man Runs 90
9. High Intensity Game Speed Build Up Play Technical Circuit 91
10. High Intensity Game Speed Build Up Play Technical Circuit (Free Decision Making) 92
11. Play Out from the Back Tactical Rotational Passing Combinations 93
12. Two Team Positional Build Up Passing Sequences 94
13. Positional and Rotational Combination Play Tactical Patterns 95
14. Positional and Rotational Combination Play Tactical Patterns with Switch of Play 96
15. Real Madrid Breaking Lines and Support Play Combinations (Variation 1) 97
16. Real Madrid Breaking Lines and Support Play Combinations (Variation 2) 98
17. Breaking Lines with Wide Combination Play Diamond Passing with Overlap 99
18. Breaking Lines with Wide Combination Play Diamond Passing with Underlap 100
19. Third Man Run Overlaps Passing Combinations with Defensive Pressure 101
20. Breaking Lines Passing Combination Waves in Pairs 102
21. Rangers FC Breaking Lines with Forward Passing Circuit 103
22. Rangers FC Breaking Lines with Dribbling Circuit + Finish 104
23. Two Way Forward Passing, Wide Combinations, and Finishing 105
24. Tactical Build Up to Break Lines and Finish Attacks (Various Patterns) 106

Advance Your Career: Become a Better Coach 107
Adam Owen Performance Consultancy 108
References 109

Dr. Adam Owen: Coach Profile
Head of Technical Development (Blackburn Rovers)

Dr. Adam Owen
UEFA Pro Coaching Licence
PhD, MPhil, BSc HONS

 @adamowen1980

 www.aoperformance.co.uk

Academic Credentials (PhD):
- Doctor of Philosophy (PhD) in Sport Science and Coaching - Claude Bernard Lyon.1 University, Lyon, France

Coaching Credentials:
- UEFA Professional Coaching Licence - Football Association of Wales (FAW)
- FA Youth Trainers Award - England Football Association (FA)

Football Positions:
- Head of Technical Development, Blackburn Rovers, England
- High-Performance and Technical Advisor, KKS Lech Poznań, Poland
- Assistant Head Coach, Hibernian FC, Scotland
- High-Performance Director and Technical Advisor, Seattle Sounders FC, USA (MLS)
- High-Performance Director and Assistant Coach, Hebei China Fortune FC, China
- Head Coach, KS Lechia Gdańsk, Poland
- High-Performance Coach, Wales National Team
- Assistant Manager, FC Servette, Switzerland
- Assistant Manager, Sheffield United FC, England
- Head of Performance, Rangers FC, Scotland
- Head of Sport Science and Fitness, Sheffield Wednesday FC, England
- Head of Academy Performance and Technical Coach, Celtic FC, Scotland
- Academy Head Coach, Wrexham FC, Wales
- Player, Wrexham FC, Wales

Further Roles, Development and Associations:

- Football Consultant, Double Pass, Belgium
- Associate Researcher (Football Science and Performance) for Lyon.1 University, France
- UEFA Professional Licence and UEFA A Licence Coach Educator for the England Football Association (FA)
- UEFA Coach Educator for various other football federations
- Faculty Member and Lecturer for the International Soccer Science and Performance Federation (ISSPF) www.ISSPF.com
- Over 100+ papers published in international peer-reviewed journals including Journals of Sport Sciences, International Journal of Sports Medicine, Journal of Strength and Conditioning Research, International Sport Science and Coaching Journal, and many more...
- Football Consultant, SL Benfica, Portugal
- Director of Research (5 years), SL Benfica, Portugal
- Key Note Speaker at various international level conferences and congresses

Dr. Adam Owen:
Career of High Performance Expert

Dr. Adam Owen has forged a distinctive blend of hands-on coaching expertise, holding a **UEFA Pro Coaching Licence**, and an esteemed academic background in Football Science and Coaching. He earned his **PhD in Sport Science & Coaching** from Lyon.1 University in France and currently serves as an associate Professor at Glyndwr University in Wales. Additionally, he maintains an associate researcher role in France while actively contributing to the professional football arena.

Adam Owen's coaching journey encompasses diverse roles across elite youth and senior levels, including **UEFA Champions League** and **Europa League** competitions, European club football, and high-profile international football engagements. Notably, at the age of 26, Adam was integral to the management team of **Rangers FC** (Scotland), reaching the **UEFA Cup Final in 2008** and staying with the club for seven and a half years. His time there yielded invaluable experience in steering the team towards successful league and cup endeavours, alongside multiple UEFA Champions League campaigns.

In 2014, Adam embraced a new challenge by joining **FC Servette** in Switzerland, marking his venture into European club football while maintaining his role with the **Wales National Team (2009-2018)**. Adam contributed to Wales' journey to the **UEFA Euro 2016 Semi-Final** in France before assuming the position of **Head Coach at Lechia Gdansk** (Poland).

Subsequently, he ventured into the Chinese Superleague as a High-Performance Director, followed by a stint with MLS Champions **Seattle Sounders FC** (USA) as Technical Advisor and High-Performance Coaching Director. His achievements include clinching the **MLS Western Conference League Title** and reaching the **MLS Cup Final**. In July 2024, Adam was appointed as **Head of Technical Development at Blackburn Rovers**. He supervises multiple departments and ensures the academy structure and approach is closely aligned with the methodology of the first team.

Adam Owen's expertise extends beyond coaching, as he also serves as an **elite coach educator at UEFA Professional level for the England FA and other UEFA federations**. As Adam's career spans playing, coaching, coach education, high-performance expertise, management, and technical directorship, he has a **unique and wide scoping expertise in the football world**.

Adam has made substantial contributions to football literature, with over 100+ publications ranging from articles, book chapters, and books. He remains actively involved in advancing football-based research at the elite level and is a faculty member of the prestigious International Soccer Science and Performance Federation (*www.ISSPF.com*), offering top-tier international online courses in football science and performance.

Drawing from his extensive domestic and international successes, Adam has developed a **research-based coaching methodology aimed at optimising individual and collective performance within elite professional football**.

How this Book Fits into the "Football Periodization to Maximise Performance" Philosophy

- The **"Football Periodization to Maximise Performance" book is a key resource**.
- The **technical practices in this book form part of this philosophy** of a full training program, so it is **highly recommended to add this book to your library**.
- Written by world leading high performance expert, **Dr. Adam Owen**, and **available from SoccerTutor.com in full colour print and eBook**.
- Proven and successful football methodology to maximise the performance of your players and team.
- Adaptable training week model for Pro, Semi-pro, Academy and Youth levels with **102 Practices** included.
- Methodological approach and training plan to produce optimum conditioning, low injury rates, and high performance.
- Make sure your players are always prepared correctly and **perform at their maximum level on match day**.

Football Periodization to Maximise Performance Methodology:

- Enhance coaches' knowledge of high performance and coaching.
- Improve player performance and gain a competitive advantage.
- Maximise the training time and efficiency of the coaching process.
- Game model: Link the technical, tactical and physical details of the game.
- Maximising the use of specific training games and practices in the training week.
- Show the actual demands imposed on players in training and manage the training load to reduce injury risk.
- How to design training sessions.
- Planning the flow of the training week to maximise performance.
- Tapering strategy = players arrive in optimal condition for the match!

Benefits of Technical Practices to Maximise Training Outcomes

Key Point

Effective technical practices are essential to a well structured football training methodology. When daily training content is poorly planned or lacks a clear methodological approach, it leads players to under perform, have inadequate conditioning, and a significantly increased risk of injury.

Recent Developments in Physical Preparation

Over the last 10 to 12 years, there has been a significant shift in how football players are physically prepared. Strength and conditioning, speed development, and high intensity, football specific endurance training have grown exponential in both understanding and implementation. These advancements have directly aligned with improvements in players' tactical awareness, technical capability, and adaptability to different systems of play.

What are the Benefits of the Technical Training in this Methodology?

- **Improved Technical Development in Players:** Structured technical practices as a bridge into the main part of the training sessions and help players become more skilled with the ball. Installing a consistent training methodology allows coaches to develop their players' technical ability.

- **Optimised Training Design:** Incorporating specific technical practices into the weekly training schedule (microcycle) ensures that sessions are highly relevant and beneficial for player development, which can be implemented into the competitive environment.

- **Enhanced Game Readiness:** Understanding tapering strategies allows coaches to fine tune training intensity and plan the involvement of technical practices to ensure players reach peak technical, physical and mental condition on match days.

- **Improve Player and Team Performance:** By integrating well planned technical practices into the overall training methodology, coaches can elevate player performance and create a more cohesive, technically proficient team.

Overall Picture of the Coaching Process: Focusing on Technical Development

Maximising the physical attributes of players is just one aspect of the performance equation. From a coach's perspective, the core objective is to build an integrated training process where the development of technical qualities is a key aspect. Achieving seamless alignment between physical conditioning, technical skills, and tactical awareness is fundamental to driving player and team progression. By prioritising the development of players' technical abilities, such as ball control, passing accuracy, and decision making, coaches can significantly elevate overall performance within the coaching process.

Technical Development in Football Periodization Methodology

The use of technical practices is widespread across all levels of football worldwide and are thoughtfully integrated into training sessions to serve a specific purpose.

Progression from Warm Up into Technical Practice

One crucial application of technical practices or blocks of work is their role as a progression from the warm up phase *(see previous book in this series: "Warm Ups to Maximise Performance")* into the main part of the coaching session. This structured approach is both functional and essential for effective training and player preparation.

A well designed technical progression serves as a vital link between the warm up phase and the demanding challenges of the main training session ahead. This progression ensures that players are mentally and physically prepared for what is next. By incorporating football specific elements during this stage of the training session, **coaches can create a smooth transition that primes the players' physically and mentally, and also aligns the practice with the technical and tactical themes of the session**. This targeted approach helps maintain a focused mindset and enhances technical repetition and development over a sustained period of time.

As highlighted in the previous book of this series (Warm Ups), the primary purpose of the warm up phase is to activate the energy systems and specific muscle groups that players will use during training. This principle extends into the technical development phase of the training session, through carefully planning and executing technical practices immediately after the warm up. Following this process in a consistent manner will ensure you as coaches can maintain the focus on preparing the players' bodies while also developing their technical skills.

Periodization Methodology

During the post-warm up phase, various technical practices are employed within a structured periodization approach or methodology. This strategic integration allows coaches to introduce specific technical actions in a controlled environment, significantly reducing the risk of injury.

Additionally, this approach enhances the players' preparedness for the more intense parts of the session. By gradually increasing the complexity and intensity of the practices, coaches can ensure that players reach a higher state of readiness, both technically and physically.

Diagram Key

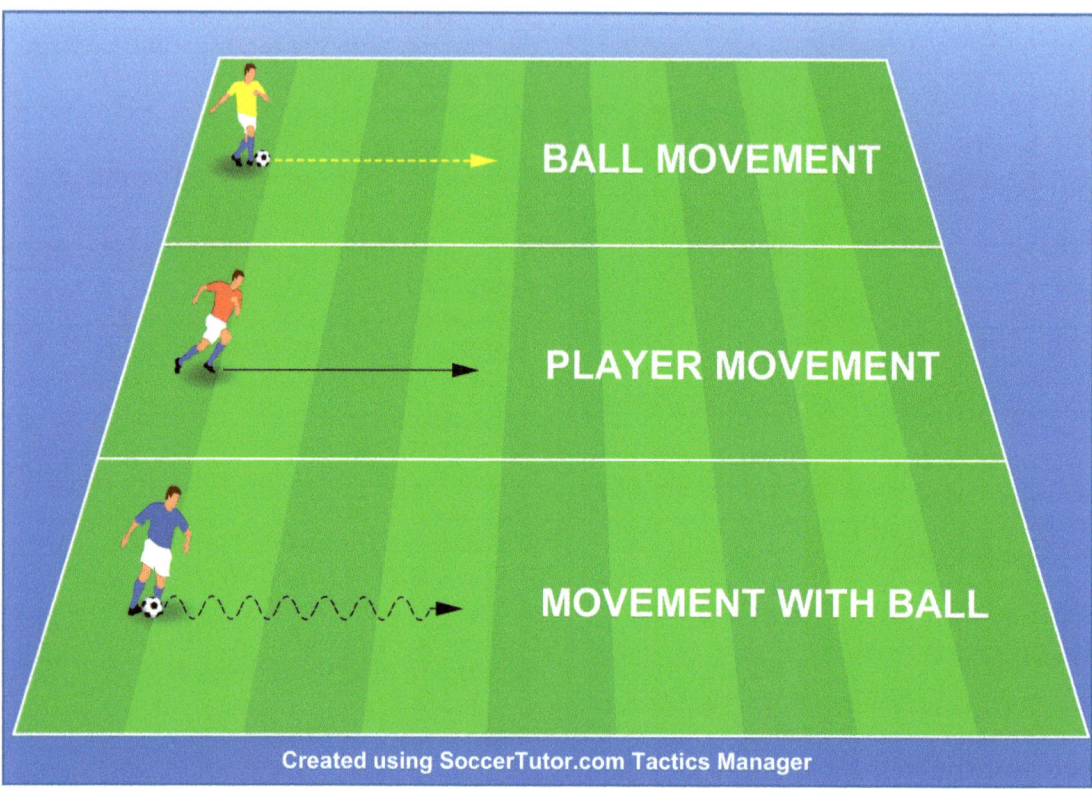

Practice Format

Each Practice includes Clear Diagrams with Supporting Training Notes:

- Name of Practice
- Practice Information and Data
- Objective of Practice
- Description of Practice
- Progressions and Coaching Points *(if applicable)*

THE TRAINING WEEK

The Training Week

Practice Design Considerations to Optimise Coaching Outcomes

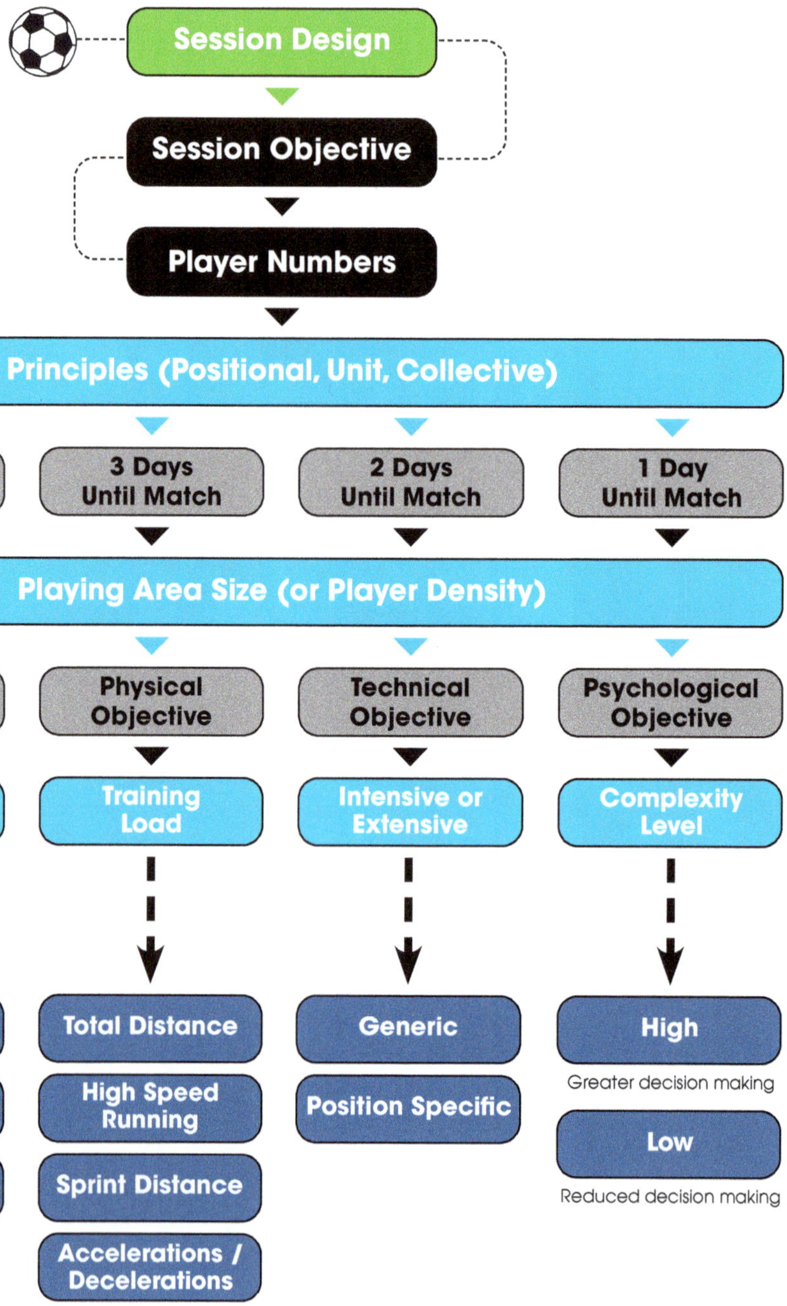

- Session Design
- Session Objective
- Player Numbers
- Principles (Positional, Unit, Collective)
  - 4 Days Until Match
  - 3 Days Until Match
  - 2 Days Until Match
  - 1 Day Until Match
- Playing Area Size (or Player Density)
  - Tactical Objective → Game Phase Focus → Attacking / Defending / Transitions
  - Physical Objective → Training Load → Total Distance / High Speed Running / Sprint Distance / Accelerations / Decelerations
  - Technical Objective → Intensive or Extensive → Generic / Position Specific
  - Psychological Objective → Complexity Level → High (Greater decision making) / Low (Reduced decision making)

Technical Practices to Maximise Performance

The Training Week

Training Session Flow

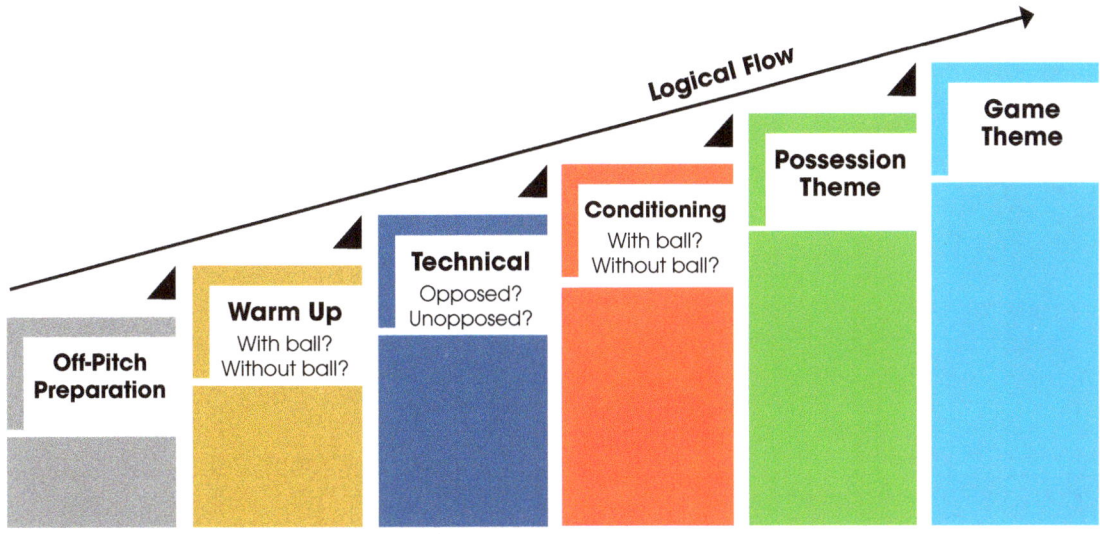

- Ensure logical flow through session – physical, technical, and tactical.
- Intelligent and efficient coaching – maintain focus and intensity.
- Be concise and direct with coaching points – maintain clarity.
- Use natural breaks to coach and get points across.
- Don't break the rhythm and reduce intensity.
- Sessions should flow!

Warm Up
- Don't just use as a time filler!
- Physically prepare for session demands.
- Psychological preparation (tactical).

Technical
- Continue flow of the session.
- Gradually increase intensity and demand from warm up phase.
- Influence technical, tactical, psychological and physical outcomes.
- Expansion or limitation of area size depending on physical requirements.

Conditioning
- Overload the physical focus of session.
- Induce key physical stimulus of session.
- Ensure opportunity for players to develop specific physical qualities.
- Prepare players fully for the upcoming intensity demands.

Possession
- Continue flow and demand of session.
- Ensure coaching within the phase is concise and intelligent, and match intensity achieves competition realism.
- Natural recovery breaks are key to minimise intensity/direction of session.

The Training Week

Planning the Training Week with Tapering Strategy to Maximise Performance

To assist in the practical application of the content, the flow of the training session is vitally important to increase the intensity, application and engagement of the players. This can be done through administering the content of the session through a logical flow, focusing on some simple key coaching points.

With good preparation, both tactically and physically, the players' roles and responsibilities can be understood further and lead to improved performances.

The following pages show you how to structure the training week (periodized microcycle) with a tapered strategy so your players can reach their peak performance.

Training week plans for Professional, Semi-professional, Youth Academy, and Grassroots (Youth) football are all included.

Periodized Practices to Maximise Performance has all different types of practices organised into their different sections:

- » **Warm Up** (Resistance, Speed Endurance, Reaction Speed)
- » **Technical** (Intensive, Extensive)
- » **Conditioning** (Resistance, Speed Endurance, Reaction Speed)
- » **Possession** (Small, Medium, Large)
- » **Game** (Small, Medium, Large)

You can then drop these practice types into the applicable day and session on the training week session plans.

The Training Week

Practical Coaching Model to Build the Training Week (Microcycle)

This page refers to the practices and physical data included in the Football Periodization to Maximise Performance book - please see page 9 for full details.

The tables to follow on pages 19-24 provide a framework for coaches of various coaching levels or categories to utilise as a guide in order to structure their training week. Following this specific training methodology, it is possible to implement an integrated training concept. Being able to understand the physical, technical and tactical outcomes of the session are key to maximising the coaching time with the players involved.

Selecting from the various categorised practices in the Football Periodization book, the warm up book, and the technical practices in this book in the correct order, provides assistance with the fundamentally important session design phase.

Furthermore, based on the understanding of the physical outcomes of each practice, **coaches will be able to enhance their knowledge of how the session design phase can be tailored to meet the session objectives from a physical, technical and tactical perspective.**

KEY POINT: Selection of practices in the three books (more volumes to follow soon) will generate a better understanding for coaches of the physical demands imposed by individual practices and accumulative total sessions over a period of time.

It should be noted that the physical data provided in the Football Periodization book practices has been generated from elite professional players, so it is suggested that practice durations, repetitions and area sizes are adapted to best suit the age groups being coached.

The data values give the readers an understanding of the demands imposed on players at the level assessed. The physical output metrics are for coaches to understand how different practices can influence different physical loads.

The 5 different training week examples (microcycles) outlined on pages 19-24 are as follows:

1. **Professional Microcycle**
   (4 Training Sessions per week + Match + Compensatory Session)

2. **Semi-professional Microcycle**
   (3 Training Sessions per week + Match)

3. **Youth Academy Microcycle**
   (2 Training Sessions per week + Match)

4. **Grassroots (Youth) Microcycle 1
   - Small Sided Game Focus**
   (1 Training Session per week, which alternates with Grassroots Microcycle 2)

5. **Grassroots (Youth) Microcycle 2
   - Large Sided Game Focus**
   (1 Training Session per week, which alternates with Grassroots Microcycle 1)

The Training Week

Periodization, Tapering Strategy, and Maximising Performance

The **Football Periodization to Maximise Performance Methodology** enables the development of a specific and integrated coaching approach to the training week, otherwise known as the **microcycle tapering strategy**.

It is well documented that placing various but contextual stressors on individual athletes or football players as a way of developing them from a physical, tactical and technical perspective is imperative. This is done through variation and changing of the training load but also ensuring the balance between work and recovery is apparent.

PERIODIZATION and TAPERING is a process of structuring and forward planning that involves the manipulation of key variables in order to cause a balanced approach to both overload and regeneration periods causing optimal performance (Mallo, 2015).

Manipulating key variables through **various constraints such as player numbers, surface area, training game types, bout duration, frequency and intensity, will** significantly affect training load variables and outcomes, which conjunctively lead to performance enhancement (Bosquet et al., 2007).

The strategy employed will be highlighted through **daily objectives or themes directly linked to their physiological focus**, whilst highlighting some of the key manipulated variables used to cause energy system and muscular overloads through football training concepts.

The practical coaching principles can be influenced by various game-model development or playing philosophies, and where possible, justify the content through published scientific work.

Please note that the training week (microcycle) overview is predominantly focusing on those starting players accumulating >45 to 60 minutes in competitive match-play. Non-starters or squad players within the group follow a program ensuring compensatory 'top-up' training is performed.

In order to understand the daily formatting, the content is titled by the number format of training days following the previous match (+), in addition to the number of days until the next fixture (-).

For example, in the Professional Microcycle (training week), the Tuesday training day is 3 days after the previous match day (previous Saturday) and 4 days before the next match day (the coming Saturday), so is therefore named **MD +3/-4**.

The Training Week

The Training Week:
Professional Microcycle

4 Training Sessions per Week + Match + Compensatory Session

DAY OF THE WEEK		MONDAY	TUESDAY	WEDNESDAY	THURSDAY	FRIDAY	SATURDAY	SUNDAY
Post-Game + / Pre-Game -		MD +2/-5	MD +3/-4	MD +4/-3	MD +5/-2	MD +6/-1	Match	MD +1/-6
Game Focus		Recovery	Intensive	Extensive	Balanced	Intensive	Extensive	Non-Starters
Tactical Focus		Evaluate	Defending	Attacking	Balanced	Review	Execute	-
PHYSICAL FOCUS		RECOVERY	RESISTANCE	SPEED END.	REACTION SPEED	ACTIVATION	MATCH	COMPENSATORY
Warm Up	Recovery	■						
	Resistance		■				■	
	Speed Endurance			■				
	Reaction Speed				■			
Technical	Intensive		■		■			
	Extensive			■				
Conditioning	Resistance		■					
	Speed Endurance			■				
	Reaction Speed				■	■		
Possession	Small Sided		■					
	Medium Sided				■			
	Large Sided			■				
Game	Small Sided			■				
	Medium Sided					■		
	Large Sided			■			■	

This example shows a specific methodology of work across the microcycle for professional or full-time training teams.

The Training Week

Training Session Format for Professional Microcycle

SUNDAY/MONDAY - 1/2 Days Until Match = Recovery

TUESDAY (70-75 min) - 4 Days Until Match (MD +3/-4)
Positional Principle Training and Resistance:

1. Resistance Warm Up (10-12 min)
2. Intensive Technical Practice (10-15 min)
3. Resistance Conditioning Practice (10-20 min)
4. Small Sided Possession (10-12 min)
5. Small Sided Game (10-25 min)

WEDNESDAY (85-95 min) - 3 Days Until Match (MD +4/-3)
Collective Team Principle Training and Speed Endurance:

1. Speed Endurance Warm Up (10-12 min)
2. Extensive Technical Practice (12-15 min)
3. Speed Endurance Conditioning Practice (5-15 min)
4. Large Sided Possession (10-15 min)
5. Large Sided Game in Large Area (10-50 min)

THURSDAY (60-70 min) - 2 Days Until Match (MD +5/-2)
Unit Principle Training and Reaction Speed Development:

1. Reaction Speed Warm Up (5-7 min)
2. Intensive Technical Practice (10-15 min)
3. Reaction Speed Conditioning Practice (5-15 min)
4. Medium Sided Possession (6-15 min)
5. Medium Sided Game (10-25 min)

FRIDAY (45-60 min) - 1 Day Until Match (MD +6/-1)
Pre-Match Activation Training Day:

1. Pre-Match Activation Warm Up (10-12 min)
2. Reaction Speed Conditioning Practice (5-15 min)
3. Large Sided Game in Small/Medium Area (10-50 min)

The Training Week

The Training Week:
Semi-Professional Microcycle

3 Training Sessions per Week + Match

DAY OF THE WEEK		MONDAY	TUESDAY	WEDNESDAY	THURSDAY	FRIDAY	SATURDAY	SUNDAY
Post-Game + / Pre-Game -		MD +2/-5	MD +3/-4	MD +4/-3	MD +5/-2	MD +6/-1	Match	MD +1/-6
Game Focus		Recovery	Intensive	Extensive	Recovery	Intensive	Extensive	Recovery
Tactical Focus		Free Evening	Defending	Attacking	Free Evening	Review	Execute	Free Evening
PHYSICAL FOCUS		RECOVERY	RESISTANCE	SPEED END.	RECOVERY	ACTIVATION	MATCH	RECOVERY
Warm Up	Recovery							
Warm Up	Resistance		■			■		
Warm Up	Speed Endurance			■				
Warm Up	Reaction Speed							
Technical	Intensive		■					
Technical	Extensive			■				
Conditioning	Resistance		■					
Conditioning	Speed Endurance			■				
Conditioning	Reaction Speed					■		
Possession	Small Sided		■					
Possession	Medium Sided							
Possession	Large Sided			■				
Game	Small Sided		■					
Game	Medium Sided						■	
Game	Large Sided			■				

This example shows a specific methodology of work across the microcycle for semi-professional teams training 3 times per week.

The Training Week

The Training Week:
Youth Academy Microcycle

2 Training Sessions per Week + Match

DAY OF THE WEEK		MONDAY	TUESDAY	WEDNESDAY	THURSDAY	FRIDAY	SATURDAY	SUNDAY
Post-Game + / Pre-Game -		MD +2/-5	MD +3/-4	MD +4/-3	MD +5/-2	MD +6/-1	Match	MD +1/-6
Game Focus		Recovery	Intensive	Recovery	Extensive	Recovery	Extensive	Recovery
Tactical Focus		Free Evening	Defending	Free Evening	Attacking	Free Evening	Execute	Free Evening
PHYSICAL FOCUS		RECOVERY	RESISTANCE	RECOVERY	SPEED END.	RECOVERY	MATCH	RECOVERY
Warm Up	Recovery							
	Resistance		■					
	Speed Endurance				■			
	Reaction Speed							
Technical	Intensive		■					
	Extensive				■			
Conditioning	Resistance		■					
	Speed Endurance				■			
	Reaction Speed							
Possession	Small Sided		■					
	Medium Sided							
	Large Sided				■			
Game	Small Sided		■					
	Medium Sided							
	Large Sided				■			

This example shows a specific methodology of work across the microcycle for youth academy teams training 2 times per week.

The Training Week

The Training Week: Grassroots (Youth) Microcycle 1

SSG/Resistance Focus - Alternates with Grassroots (Youth) Microcycle 2

DAY OF THE WEEK		MONDAY	TUESDAY	WEDNESDAY	THURSDAY	FRIDAY	SATURDAY	SUNDAY
Post-Game + / Pre-Game -		MD +2/-5	MD +3/-4	MD +4/-3	MD +5/-2	MD +6/-1	Match	MD +1/-6
Game Focus		Recovery	Recovery	Extensive	Recovery	Recovery	Extensive	Recovery
Tactical Focus		Free Evening	Free Evening	Defending	Free Evening	Free Evening	Execute	Free Evening
PHYSICAL FOCUS		RECOVERY	RECOVERY	SPEED END.	RECOVERY	RECOVERY	MATCH	RECOVERY
Warm Up	Recovery							
	Resistance			■				
	Speed Endurance							
	Reaction Speed							
Technical	Intensive			■				
	Extensive							
Conditioning	Resistance			■				
	Speed Endurance							
	Reaction Speed							
Possession	Small Sided			■				
	Medium Sided							
	Large Sided							
Game	Small Sided			■				
	Medium Sided							
	Large Sided							

Grassroots (Youth) Microcycle 1 has a small sided game focus and alternates with Grassroots (Youth) Microcycle 2 - <u>see next page</u>, which has a large sided game focus.

Technical Practices to Maximise Performance

The Training Week

The Training Week:
Grassroots (Youth) Microcycle 2

LSG/Speed Endurance Focus - Alternates with Grassroots (Youth) Microcycle 1

DAY OF THE WEEK		MONDAY	TUESDAY	WEDNESDAY	THURSDAY	FRIDAY	SATURDAY	SUNDAY
Post-Game + / Pre-Game -		MD +2/-5	MD +3/-4	MD +4/-3	MD +5/-2	MD +6/-1	Match	MD +1/-6
Game Focus		Recovery	Recovery	Extensive	Recovery	Recovery	Extensive	Recovery
Tactical Focus		Free Evening	Free Evening	Defending	Free Evening	Free Evening	Execute	Free Evening
PHYSICAL FOCUS		RECOVERY	RECOVERY	SPEED END.	RECOVERY	RECOVERY	MATCH	RECOVERY
Warm Up	Recovery							
	Resistance							
	Speed Endurance			■				
	Reaction Speed							
Technical	Intensive							
	Extensive			■				
Conditioning	Resistance							
	Speed Endurance			■				
	Reaction Speed							
Possession	Small Sided							
	Medium Sided							
	Large Sided			■				
Game	Small Sided							
	Medium Sided							
	Large Sided			■				

Grassroots (Youth) Microcycle 2 has a large sided game focus and alternates with Grassroots (Youth) Microcycle 1 - <u>see previous page</u>, which has a small sided game focus.

The Training Week

Analysis of a 6-Week Training Mesocycle and Positional Quantification in Elite European Football Players

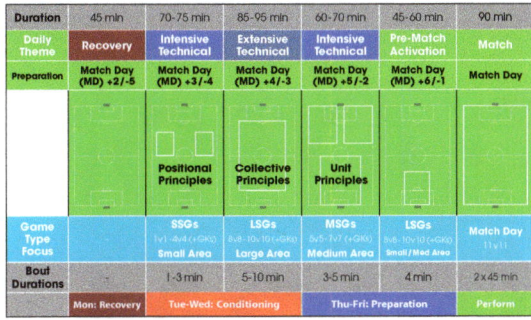

What?

Analyse a training mesocycle whilst quantifying positional demands imposed on elite European football players.

When?

Data recorded from players across a 6-week in-season training mesocycle period.

How?

- Daily **GPS** and **rating of perceived exertion (RPE)** load recorded.
- Metrics included: **Total distance** (m), **high-intensity distance** (m), **sprint distance** (m), **average speed** (m.min), **RPE load** (RPE x duration).
- **Positional demands** and **training loads** analysed in addition with match conditions (i.e. match location and match score), as well as player's age.

Who?

16 elite male European football players participated in the study.

Results?

- **Training Loads:** Typical daily training loads did not differ throughout each week of the in-season mesocycle. Total Load (TL) significantly reduced on MD-1 vs. TLs on MD-2, MD-3 and MD-4 preceding a match.
- Physical output differences found between MD-2, MD-3, and MD-4 revealed a structured, tapering approach to microcycle.
- **Positional: WFs =>** Total distance and Very High Intensity Running (VHIR) distance vs. other positions; **CBs** = significantly less < Total Distance (TD) and VHIR vs. other positions.
- Reduced average speeds (metres per min) reported in training sessions post-successful matches vs. post-defeats (p<0.05).
- Reduced average speeds (metres per min) also reported post-away fixtures vs. home fixtures within the microcycle.

Practical Application?

- Coaches can maintain a uniformed and structured training load mesocycle whilst inducing variation of the physical outputs during the microcycle phase.
- Additionally, the investigation also provides a tapering approach that may induce significant variation of the positional demands.

Full Scientific Reference

Owen AL., Lago-Penas C., Gomez AM., Mendes B., Dellal A. (2017).
Analysis of a Training Mesocycle & Positional Quantification in Elite European Soccer Players | International Journal of Sport Science & Coaching, DOI: 10.1177/1747954117727851

PERIODIZATION OF TECHNICAL TRAINING

Periodization of Technical Practices in Football Training

The periodization of technical practices is vital in football training, helping players develop essential skills while experiencing a gradual progression that mirrors match intensity. This approach transitions players smoothly through training phases, from the warm up to focused technical work and game specific practices. The aim is to ensure a seamless flow, enhancing both the technical development and physical readiness of the players.

Transition from Warm Up to Technical Phase

The warm up phase is the foundation of any training session. The primary aim is to prepare the players physically, activating them from a physical and psychological perspective while increasing their heart rates and blood flow **(see previous book in this series: "Warm Ups to Maximise Performance")**. In the context of periodized technical practices, the warm up should also serve as a bridge to the next stage: **The Technical Phase**.

In the pre-technical phase, it is essential to replicate movements that players will later execute during possession games, conditioning, or game related practices. For example, warm ups that involve light passing, receiving, and scanning not only prepare the muscles but also engage the players' technical awareness and decision making processes. These movements should mirror the specific demands of the technical practice to follow, ensuring a gradual transition and avoiding significant elevations or changes in intensity and demand.

Technical Development

The technical phase of the session has two main aims:

1. *Developing players' technical skills*.
2. *Preparing players for the mental and physical demands of the entire training session*.

Repetition of key actions, such as body positioning, scanning, and decision making, is essential, developing muscle memory and mental readiness so players can then execute under pressure.

This phase also **safely elevates physical intensity through short, sharp passes, quick direction changes, and controlled ball striking**. By progressively increasing intensity of the practices, players' muscles are gradually prepared for higher intensity movements in game-like situations, helping to reduce the risk of injury.

Psychological and Cognitive Preparation

Technical practices are not just about skill execution - they also provide an opportunity to enhance mental processes. Through decision making scenarios and scanning exercises, players become aware of passing options, player movements and how to make the correct technical decisions at match speed. This aspect is critical in preparing them for the decision heavy demands of possession or game related practices later in the session. **Body shape, timing of passes, and awareness of teammates' positioning are all practiced to create a technical readiness for the session**.

Periodization of Technical Training

Intensive and Extensive Technical Practices

In the context of the **Football Periodization to Maximise Performance methodology (see pages 9-10 for full details)**, the technical practices are categorised into intensive and extensive based on the physical demands and the technical skills they aim to develop.

INTENSIVE Technical Practices

These practices focus on **shorter distances**, both in terms of passing and running. The aim is to **develop quick and explosive movements that closely mimic high speed and intensity actions** that occur during specific moments of matches, such as in tight spaces or high pressure situations.

Intensive Technical Practices involve:

- *Short, sharp passes*.
- *Quick changes of direction*.
- *Explosive acceleration over short distances*.

Intensive technical practices align with small and medium sided games, which are on the **MD +3/-4 and MD +5/-2 training days in elite professional football (see pages 19-20 for details)**. Intensive practices overload the muscles in a way that focuses on explosiveness, muscle reactivity, and fine motor skills. The shorter durations and high frequency of technical actions also reinforce rapid decision-making and technical execution in confined spaces, enhancing players' speed of play.

EXTENSIVE Technical Practices

Extensive technical practices involve **larger distances** to execute technical actions and **more physically demanding actions**.

Extensive Technical Practices involve:

- **Longer passes**.
- **High-speed running**.
- **Near sprinting speeds**.
- **Large sided games** are the focus of the latter stage of the training week (microcycle) strategy in terms of game stimulus, so extensive technical practices align with the MD +5/-2 training day.

The aim is to prepare players for situations where **longer sprints, more extensive ball movements**, and **longer technical actions** e.g. switching play, playing forward, line breaking passes. This overloads the muscles differently, placing **emphasis on speed endurance and sustained larger distance technical executions at high speeds**. These practices are essential for game scenarios where players must maintain physicality and technical accuracy in more expansive playing areas.

Periodizing technical practices with a clear progression, from warm up to game related practices, **ensures players are developing technically and are prepared physically and psychologically for the demands of the match**. Technical phases within training activate the body and **prime the mind** through repeated, targeted actions that mirror the subsequent phases of play. By using intensive and extensive technical practices, coaches **develop both explosive actions and sustained speed** (or endurance), ensuring players are well prepared for the full range of demands they will encounter on the pitch later in the training session.

Intensive and Extensive Technical Passing Actions in Football

When researching around technical or passing activities within football, the experts define certain types of passes into short, medium and long:

- **Short Passes**
  5-15 yards (4.5-14 metres)
- **Medium Passes**
  15-30 yards (14-27 metres)
- **Long Passes**
  30+ yards (27+ metres)

This enables analysis of the technical passing analysis per player and team which may highlight key findings from specific systems and styles of play.

According to the passing and technical analysis research by Cordón-Carmona et al. (2023), **teams in the top five (men's) European leagues tend to prioritise short, ground passes** while quickly integrating other types of passes. However, coaches should not overlook the importance of incorporating long and high passes, even if they are used less frequently during matches. Effective practice of these passes can surprise opponents and enhance overall team performance.

In elite professional football, passing is a critical aspect of competitive matches and all training sessions. It is **essential for coaches to train players to develop the technical action of passing through the repetition of learning**, then enhance these technical skills within realistic or game-like situations. By incorporating decision making into possession and game-based training methods, **coaches can help players refine the technical skills needed for different types of passes**, ultimately enhancing their team's effectiveness and success.

Within this book and methodology of training, technical actions are categorised into two distinct types:

1. **INTENSIVE Technical Actions**
2. **EXTENSIVE Technical Actions**

These classifications enable coaches to design training sessions that closely replicate the demands of match play, ensuring a well rounded development of players' skills and physical abilities.

The **categorisation of technical actions into intensive and extensive allows for a structured and strategic approach to training on the correct days of the training week (microcycle)**, and also enables coaches to understand how they can link their training practices to the game based strategy.

By understanding and applying these distinctions, coaches can create training sessions that not only prepare players for the varied demands of match play but also ensure a balanced development of their technical and physical skills.

Periodization of Technical Training

Considerations of the Microcycle (Training Week)

Duration	45 min	70-75 min	85-95 min	60-70 min	45-60 min	90 min
Daily Theme	Recovery	Intensive Technical	Extensive Technical	Intensive Technical	Pre-Match Activation	Match
Preparation	Match Day (MD) +2/-5	Match Day (MD) +3/-4	Match Day (MD) +4/-3	Match Day (MD) +5/-2	Match Day (MD) +6/-1	Match Day
		Positional Principles	Collective Principles	Unit Principles		
Game Type Focus	-	SSGs 1v1-4v4 (+GKs) Small Area	LSGs 8v8-10v10 (+GKs) Large Area	MSGs 5v5-7v7 (+GKs) Medium Area	LSGs 8v8-10v10 (+GKs) Small/Med Area	Match Day 11v11
Bout Durations	-	1-3 min	5-10 min	3-5 min	4 min	2 x 45 min
	Mon: Recovery	Tue-Wed: Conditioning		Thu-Fri: Preparation		Perform

When working within a specific coaching strategy or microcycle, which includes multiple training sessions throughout the week, it is essential to adopt a strategic and well balanced approach to progressing from the warm up phase into the main session theme. **Incorporating intensive or extensive technical practices into this transition is critical for both reducing injury risk and maximising performance** and training outcomes.

By utilising specific technical development practices that align with the physical, technical, and psychological objectives of each session, **coaches can establish a consistent training flow**, improve precision, and introduce necessary variability. This not only optimises performance but also significantly contributes to **injury prevention**, as it ensures that players are progressively prepared for the physical demands of the session.

To truly optimise session strategy, player fitness, and readiness to train, the transition from warm up to the main coaching theme must be progressive. The use of the correct technical development practices between the warm up phase and the conditioning, or possession theme are scheduled according to the theme of the training day.

Integrating the correct intensive and extensive technical practices on the right day as part of a progressive training routine supports both performance enhancement and long term physical well-being.

PASSING ANALYSIS: HIGHLIGHTING THE TECHNICAL REQUIREMENTS OF ELITE PLAYERS

Passing Analysis: Highlighting the Technical Requirements of Elite Players

Technical Passing Performance of Elite Midfielder Rodri (Ballon d'Or Winner)

Completed Passes and Distances (2023/24 Season)

Rodri (Manchester City Midfielder) Passing Statistics						
2023/24 Season (Premier League)	Min	Passes Attempted	Passes Completed	Pass Completion %	Total Passing Distance (yards)	Progressive Passing Distance
Match 1	90	110	107	97 %	1679	463
Match 2	90	135	122	90 %	1964	638
Match 3	90	119	114	96 %	2147	487
Match 4	75	92	85	92 %	1527	373
Match 5	90	116	113	97 %	1943	542
Match 6	82	100	92	89 %	1640	460
Match 7	45	78	75	96 %	1279	311
Match 8	90	118	107	91 %	2069	517
Match 9	90	89	83	93 %	1595	374
Match 10	89	110	103	94 %	2193	564
Match 11	90	90	80	89 %	1416	402
Match 12	70	99	94	95 %	1683	498
Match 13	90	76	67	88 %	1246	335
Match 14	90	102	97	95 %	1878	534
Match 15	90	152	141	93 %	2306	604
Match 16	90	76	69	91 %	1387	370
Match 17	90	96	87	91 %	1137	286
Match 18	90	106	90	85 %	1523	331
Match 19	90	123	115	94 %	2101	565
Match Average	85	105	97	92 &	1722	455

Rodri's (Manchester City/Spain) passing statistics across 19 Premier League matches provide an insight into his pivotal role as a defensive midfielder.

His general passing performance was consistently high with an **average total of 97 completed passes**, peaking at 141, and a **92% completion rate**, reflecting his reliability in possession.

Rodri's average total passing distance was 1722 yards (1575 metres), which shows significant involvement in maintaining and distributing possession.

Rodri's average progressive passing distance was 455 yards (416 metres), which highlights his effectiveness in advancing the ball and contributing to the team's attacking play.

Passing Analysis: Highlighting the Technical Requirements of Elite Players

Rodri's Short Passing (2023/24 Season)

Short Passes (5-15 yards)				
2023/24 Season (Selected 19 Matches)	Min	Passes Attempted	Passes Completed	Pass Completion %
Match 1	90	55	55	100 %
Match 2	90	69	66	96 %
Match 3	90	41	40	98 %
Match 4	75	40	38	95 %
Match 5	90	56	54	96 %
Match 6	82	53	48	91 %
Match 7	45	38	37	97 %
Match 8	90	38	36	95 %
Match 9	90	32	28	88 %
Match 10	89	29	28	97 %
Match 11	90	45	39	87 %
Match 12	70	45	44	98 %
Match 13	90	36	29	81 %
Match 14	90	36	36	100
Match 15	90	70	68	97 %
Match 16	90	26	25	96 %
Match 17	90	60	60	100 %
Match 18	90	56	49	88 %
Match 19	90	55	53	96 %
Match Average	**85**	**46**	**44**	**95 %**

KEY:

- **Short Passes**
  5-15 yards (4.5-14 metres)
- **Medium Passes**
  15-30 yards (14-27 metres)
- **Long Passes**
  30+ yards (27+ metres)

Short Passes

When analysing Rodri's passing performance, his short passing was executed with near perfect precision.

He had an **average completion rate of 95%**, including a flawless 100% in two matches.

Passing Analysis: Highlighting the Technical Requirements of Elite Players

Rodri's Medium and Long Passes (2023/24 Season)

Medium Passes (15-30 yards)			Long Passes (30+ yards)		
Passes Attempted	Passes Completed	Pass Completion %	Passes Attempted	Passes Completed	Pass Completion %
42	41	98 %	8	7	88 %
48	41	85 %	11	9	82 %
61	60	98 %	14	12	86 %
37	35	95 %	12	10	83 %
50	49	98 %	9	9	100 %
37	32	87 %	12	12	100 %
32	30	94 %	7	7	100 %
66	60	91 %	14	11	79 %
40	39	98 %	14	14	100 %
61	57	93 %	17	16	94 %
30	28	93 %	12	11	92 %
39	36	92 %	13	13	100 %
29	29	100 %	10	9	99 %
49	47	96 %	13	13	100 %
69	65	94 %	10	6	60 %
32	29	91 %	15	13	87 %
26	22	85 %	5	2	40 %
38	34	90 %	11	7	64 %
46	44	96 %	20	17	85 %
44	**41**	**93 %**	**12**	**10**	**86 %**

* Data listed is from Match 1 to Match 19 like on previous page (last row shows the Match Averages)

Medium Passes

Rodri's completion rate was an incredible 93%.

Long Passes

Even with long passes, which are much more difficult, Rodri still had an **extremely high completion rate of 86%.**

Rodri's passing versatility enables him to adapt seamlessly to tactical demands. His progressive passing distance highlights his ability to move the ball forward, break lines, and initiate attacks.

With high completion rates across all passing ranges and types, he is pivotal in maintaining possession and in transitions from defence to attack, making him an indispensable asset to his team.

Passing Analysis: Highlighting the Technical Requirements of Elite Players

Technical Passing in Football: Lessons from Rodri's Elite Performance

Case Study: Balancing Intensive and Extensive Passing

To illustrate the coaching approach for developing technically efficient players with superior passing execution, we examined the passing data of **Spanish Ballon d'Or winning Manchester City defensive midfielder Rodri**. His performances highlight the **critical balance between intensive (short, high frequency) and extensive (longer range, expansive) passing**. Rodri's ability to execute both types of passes under varying levels of pressure underscores the importance of technical precision and decision making in match play.

Modern Passing Dynamics

In today's game, the ability to transition seamlessly between short, intensive passes and long, extensive passes is vital for maintaining possession and exploiting space. Rodri demonstrates excellence in this regard, frequently completing intricate short combinations in tight spaces to advance play and initiate attacks. Simultaneously, he delivers precise diagonal or vertical passes to switch play, break lines, and launch counter attacks. His mastery of these skills reflects the demands of modern football, where versatility and adaptability in passing are of paramount importance.

Developing Elite Passing Skills: Two-Pronged Approach

For aspiring players and coaches, replicating technical passing skills like Rodri's requires a structured training foundation. This involves **deliberate practice through a combination of unopposed and opposed practices**. Unopposed practices focus on refining technique in isolated settings, enabling consistency and precision. Opposed practices, on the other hand, introduce game-like pressure, simulating match situations that challenge players to adapt quickly and make effective decisions.

Rodri's example serves as a benchmark for how **technical excellence is not merely innate talent but the result of intentional, structured development**. Coaches must prioritise varied, game-relevant repetitions to cultivate players who are not only technically proficient but also tactically aware and confident in dynamic situations. By doing so, they can prepare players to achieve the precision and adaptability characteristic of elite footballers like Rodri.

Passing Analysis: Highlighting the Technical Requirements of Elite Players

Passing Dominance in La Liga: Real Madrid and Barcelona

Small (Navy), Medium (Black), and Long Passes (Grey) - Totals During 2023/24 La Liga Season

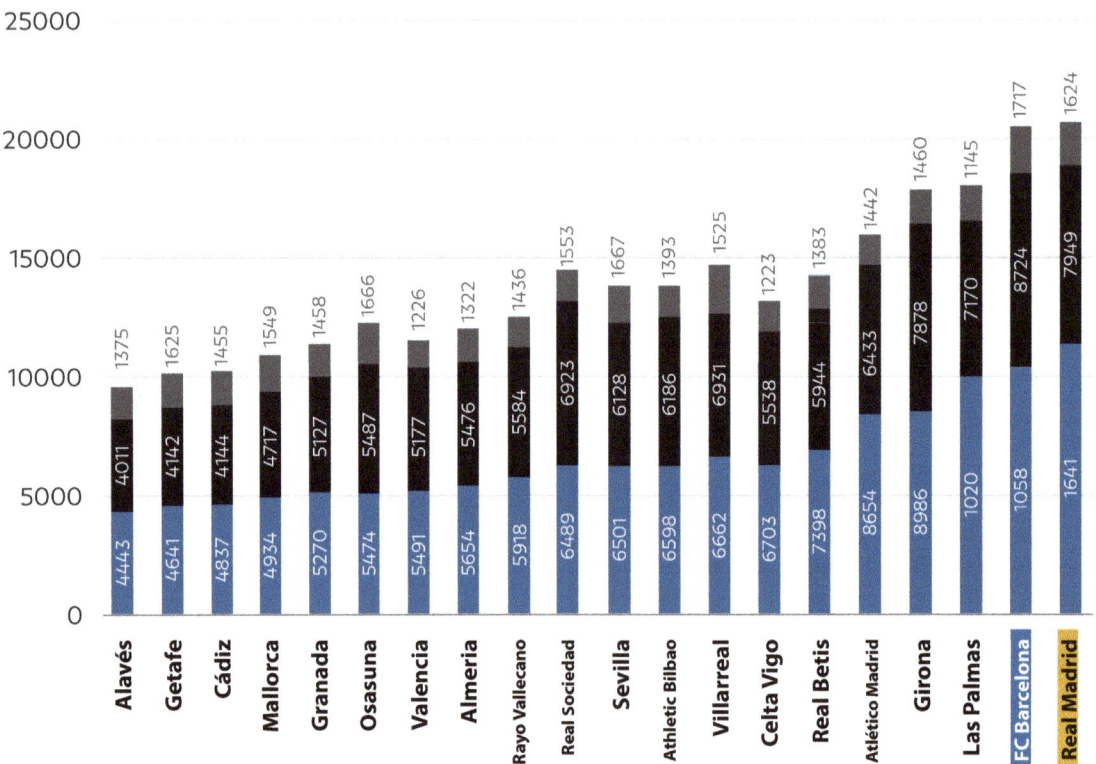

An analysis of the Spanish La Liga 2023/2024 season reveals how the two giants of the league, **Real Madrid** and **FC Barcelona**, **dominate in small and medium length passes compared to other teams**.

While their possession dominance might initially suggest a higher number of passes overall, the tactical and technical nuance lies in their reliance on shorter passing distances.

This approach ensures that players are consistently positioned close to the ball, enabling them to quickly regain possession if lost. Additionally, the exceptional positional play and technical quality of their players likely contribute significantly to their ability to outplay opponents and maintain control of the game. This combination of **precise, short passing and intelligent positioning underpins their consistent dominance in La Liga**.

Passing Analysis: Highlighting the Technical Requirements of Elite Players

Analysis of Passing and Goal Scoring Trends at International Tournaments

Euro 2016: Passing and Scoring Trends

Data from Euro 2016 revealed no significant differences in pass length categorised as short (0-17m), medium (17-34m), and long (34m+) between teams that advanced from the group stage and those that did not. However, an important observation was that the **likelihood of scoring decreased as the number of long passes increased**.

World Cup 2014: The Role of Medium Length Passes

During the 2014 World Cup, **22.2% of goals were scored from passes (assists) ranging between 10-24m**. This finding highlights the **critical role medium length passes played in goal scoring situations** during the tournament.

Euro 2016: Goal Distribution by Pass Length

An analysis of goals scored in Euro 2016 revealed that 18.4% came from passes longer than 10m, while 17.1% originated from passes shorter than 10m. This **slight advantage for longer passes suggests a preference for bypassing defenders with decisive passes in key moments**.

Spain's World Cup 2010 Triumph: Short Passing Dominance

Spain's World Cup winning campaign in 2010 demonstrated the dominance of a short passing strategy. Their ability to maintain possession and build attacks through **concise and precise passing underpinned their success**.

Key Conclusions for Coaches

These insights emphasise the **value of incorporating a balanced passing strategy in training**. While short passes are essential for maintaining possession, especially in a style like Spain's, medium length passes have proven to be highly effective in creating scoring opportunities. Long passes, while occasionally useful, are less reliable for goal scoring.

How this Book Can Help Coaches

The **50 intensive (short distances) and extensive (larger distances) technical practices in the book provide a comprehensive methodology for training players to develop their short and medium length passing**.

By implementing these practices into your training sessions, you the coach, can effectively **prepare your teams to maximise attacking efficiency and achieve success in competitive matches**.

Breaking Lines and Passing Distances

The Importance of Passing in Goal Creation

In football, nearly every goal, excluding set pieces like direct free kicks and penalties, involves at least one pass. This highlights the **crucial need for precise execution and coordination among teammates**. Accurate passing ensures the ball reaches its intended recipient, maintains possession, and creates scoring opportunities.

Direct Play vs Possession Based Strategies

Research by Reep & Benjamin indicates that **80% of goals result from three passes or fewer, highlighting the effectiveness of direct play**. Meanwhile, Hughes & Frank found that successful teams generate more shots per possession during longer passing sequences than shorter ones. However, the conversion **ratio of shots to goals remains higher for direct play than possession based approaches**.

Successful teams show adaptability by varying their passing sequences based on the specific match situations, enabling them to exploit tactical opportunities and remain effective overall.

Positioning, Line Breaking, and Diagonal Runs

The quickest way to advance the ball towards the goal is through effective passing that bypasses defenders or breaks defensive lines (line breaking passes).

When a player has possession, their objective should be to receive the ball in the most advantageous position. Their **advantage can improve by 7% if the player separates from the nearest defender and teammates or by 5% if they move towards the ball** upon receiving it.

FIFA states, "line breaks are one of the most important events in football, occurring when the attacking team moves the ball beyond the deepest opposition player in a unit." A **diagonal run by the receiver increases the success rate of completing the play, resulting in a goal, shot on target, or free kick by 7%**. Whether executing an organised attack, counter attack, or short attack, the success of these plays is closely tied to passing accuracy.

Intensive and Extensive Passing in Training Sessions

For coaches, this underscores the importance of training players to position themselves strategically and pass precisely. Practicing these techniques leads to more effective scoring opportunities in matches.

It is extremely **important to practice both intensive short, precise passing exchanges in tight spaces and extensive passing, which involves longer passes to exploit space and disrupt the opposition's defensive organisation**.

Incorporating these practices into training enhances players' technical skills, decision making, and tactical understanding, equipping them to handle the game's dynamic demands while contributing to the team's success.

Passing Analysis: Highlighting the Technical Requirements of Elite Players

Breaking Defensive Lines: Insights from Argentina's World Cup Final vs France (18th Dec 2022)

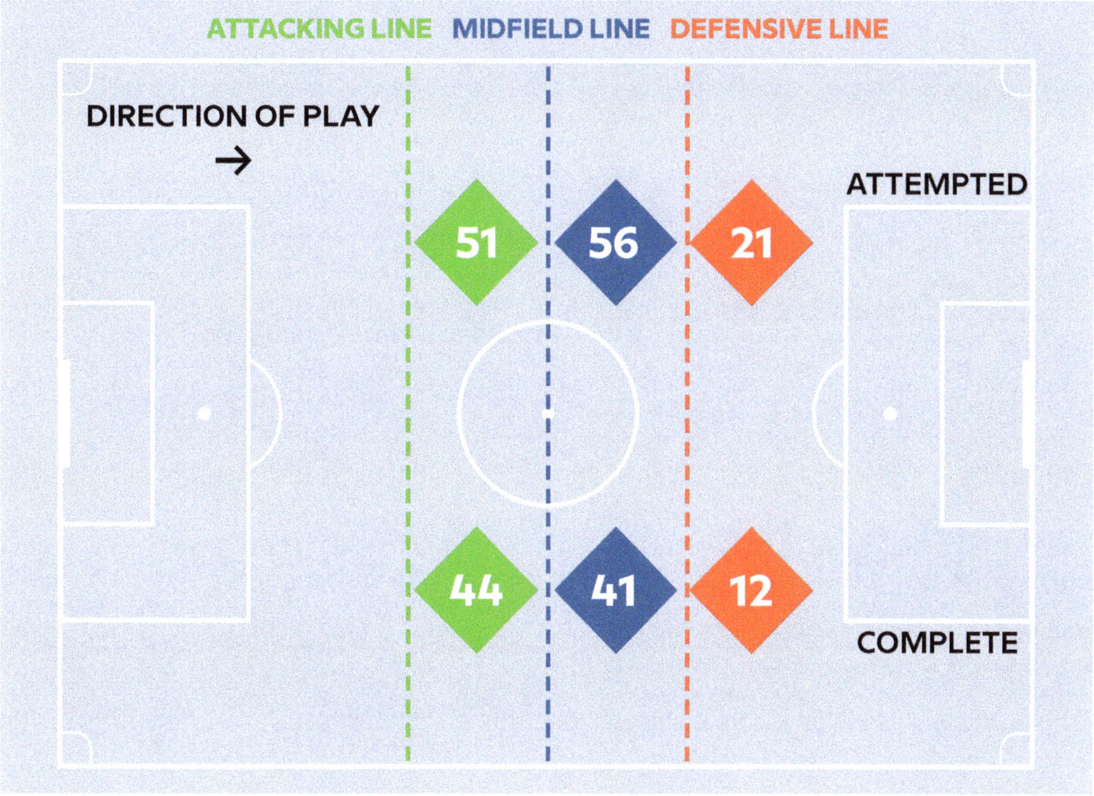

ATTACKING LINE **MIDFIELD LINE** **DEFENSIVE LINE**

DIRECTION OF PLAY →

ATTEMPTED: 51 | 56 | 21

COMPLETE: 44 | 41 | 12

Passing Distance to Break Lines and Success Rate

The diagram shows Argentina's advancing play against France's defensive structure (three lines) in the 2022 World Cup Final. The distances needed to break through France's lines relative to the dimensions of the pitch are shown, reinforcing the value of technical activities in player development. Argentina attempted 51 passes to break one line of defence, completing 44 successfully. They attempted 56 passes to break two lines, completing 41, and finally they attempted 21 passes to break three lines, completing 12.

Success Rate (%) of Short, Medium, and Long Passes

- The **shorter passes through a single defensive line** had the highest success rate (**86%**).
- The **medium passes attempting to break two lines** carried greater risk (**73%**).
- The **longer passes attempting to break three lines** (**57%**) proved far less successful.

Note: These insights help coaches design training practices that simulate the challenges of breaking defensive lines effectively and efficiently.

Tactical Insights and Practical Applications for Coaches

Emphasise Patience in Build Up Play

Encourage players to adopt a patient approach in advancing the ball, prioritising horizontal movement and careful ball retention. Players should **focus on waiting for the opportune moment to break through the opposition's lines**, ensuring the attack is deliberate and calculated. This method not only minimises the risk of losing possession but also provides greater control over the tempo of the game.

Incorporate Long Passing Sequences

Training sessions should regularly include practices that replicate longer passing sequences. These practices **help players build their ability to maintain possession and progress the ball effectively over extended periods**. The focus should be on developing both accuracy and composure during these sequences, and developing player confidence in high pressure situations where patience is critical.

Penetrating Through Passes

Coaches should **emphasise the importance of through passes** and other penetrating passes. However, a balanced approach is necessary to allow teams to adapt their attacking strategies to exploit specific weaknesses in the opposition's defensive organisation. Coaches should tailor their training practices to align with their team's overall playing style and the tactical challenges posed by different types of opponents.

Adapting to Match Situations

Coaches should prioritise training players to adapt their passing strategies according to different situations they will encounter in a match. For example, **when facing a compact defence, players need to rely on precise passes and off the ball movement to break down the block**. When losing in a game, players should be prepared to execute more direct and aggressive passes to regain momentum and create goal scoring opportunities.

Conclusion

By adopting a more patient and structured approach to build up play, your team will achieve greater success in attack. Coaches should emphasise the technical and tactical requirements of elite football to elevate their team's match day performance.

Furthermore, the variety of technical actions executed by top level players demonstrates the need for coaches to introduce regular periodized technical practices.

This book highlights the **importance of incorporating both intensive (short distances) and extensive (longer distances) passing practices into your training sessions to prepare players for the demands of competition**.

Further Technical Research Findings in Elite Professional Football

Slower Progression: A Mark of Top Teams

Research by González-Rodenas et al. (2023) highlights that **higher ranked teams in elite football progress the ball at a slower speed** compared to lower ranked teams. This deliberate approach highlights their **patience in build up play**, characterised by horizontal ball movement and longer passing sequences. These teams **carefully wait for the right moments to break through opposing lines**, showing consistency regardless of match location, opponent quality, or outcome. In contrast, lower ranked teams tend to rely heavily on counter attacks or rapid changes in play to advance quickly towards the goal. This explains their higher speed of progression but often reduced ball possession and fewer controlled attacks.

Attacking Strategy: Penetrating Passes

Despite their slower forward progression, **top teams cover more ground per sequence and make more frequent and decisive entries into the final third**. This reflects a sophisticated attacking strategy, highlighted by an **increased use of crosses and through passes to penetrate their opponent's defensive structure**. Such tactics are very effective against low block defences, where breaking lines requires precision and variety in passing.

Crosses vs Through Passes

Some research suggests that penetrating passes, such as through passes may have a higher success rate than crosses delivered from wide areas. For instance, Lago-Peñas et al. found that winning teams delivered fewer crosses but conceded more, while Zhou et al. observed that teams in the Chinese Super League crossed more frequently when they were losing. On the other hand, Casal et al. reported that effective crosses were instrumental in attacking success in La Liga. Similarly, a study from the German Bundesliga demonstrated a clear relationship between the number of crosses and total points earned across the season.

These findings offer invaluable insights for coaches, reinforcing the importance of a flexible attacking strategy. Training should incorporate crossing and focus on through passes and other penetrating passes to ensure players are equipped to exploit different types of defensive organisations. By blending these approaches, teams can enhance their ability to adapt to different match situations and improve their overall effectiveness in breaking down opposition defences.

Passing Analysis: Highlighting the Technical Requirements of Elite Players

Impact of Player Movements When Receiving Passes (La Liga Study)

Zones of the Pitch (for reference)

Figure adapted from Cordón-Carmona et al., (2020) and Fernandez-Navarro et al., (2020).

Direction of Play

Defensive Zone	Pre-Defensive Zone	Pre-Attacking Zone	Attacking Zone
5	10	15	20
4	9	14	19
3	8	13	18
2	7	12	17
1	6	11	16

Research by Cordón-Carmona et al. (2020) on elite La Liga players identifies new metrics for evaluating passing effectiveness and combination success.

The findings emphasise the importance of player movements when receiving, indicating that **the space where a pass is received and a receiver's movement (diagonal or vertical) positively influence successful outcomes**.

Furthermore, the **pitch zone of pass origin (pre-attack or attack) strongly impacts effectiveness**. Although pass angle shows a weaker correlation with success, it remains crucial for space creation and progression in play.

Passing Analysis: Highlighting the Technical Requirements of Elite Players

Summary of the La Liga Study Findings

For coaches to enhance their team's attack completion effectiveness, consider these key study findings (refer to zone diagram on previous page).

Study Findings

- As highlighted by a study of Spain's La Liga, **successful passes in the Pre-Attack and Attack Zones 11 to 20 significantly increase the likelihood of concluding a passage of play with a shot on goal**.
- Interestingly, while the Wide Left Pre-Attack Zone 15 showed a slight reduction in passing success rate (0.6%), this was due to the higher effectiveness of passes from the Central Pre-Attack Zone 13 and Wide Right Pre-Attack Zone 11.
- The Central Pre-Defensive Zone 8 recorded the highest total number of passes, followed by Central Pre-Attack Zone 13 and Wide Right Pre-Attack Zone 11, underscoring the strategic importance of these areas in playmaking.
- **Diagonal passing and movements to create space and receive the ball are shown to lead to greater ball retention, and therefore more chances created, and more goals scored!**

Conclusion and How this Book Can Help Coaches

To emphasise the importance of varying technical passing development from a player's perspective, **coaches should recognise the value of exposing players to diverse passing practices that incorporate variations in distance, speed, and angles**. These variations help players adapt and generate success for their team in dynamic match scenarios.

While teams differ in their playing styles, as do their opponents' defensive strategies, the consistent **need for players to develop versatile passing skills** remains crucial. Coaches must therefore look to design practices that mirror these findings, **encouraging their players to adapt and execute effective passes in various pitch zones** to optimise team performance.

In relation to the findings that diagonal passes and movements improve success rates, this research can be used by coaches to think about not only developing the type of technical considerations needed when building practices and sessions, but also to think about the passer and receiving players' movements (vertical, horizontal vs diagonal). Coaches can implement these findings into their training to maximise players' technical development and refine tactical approaches.

Emphasising player movement in strategic zones and focusing on maintaining possession in key areas can significantly improve attacking efficiency and match outcomes. These insights can guide coaches and coaching staff to focus on the types of runs or movements of players during an attack, emphasising movements that create useful spaces and enhance the chances of reaching the goal.

NOTE: This book offers a variety of practices centred on these principles, ready to be integrated into your training to enhance player development and improve team performance.

INTENSIVE TECHNICAL PRACTICES (SMALL SPACES)

Intensive Technical Actions and Practices in Small Spaces

Intensive technical actions are characterised by their short, sharp nature, and minimal recovery time between activities.

Intensive technical actions are designed to **replicate the high intensity, quick decision making situations players encounter during a match**.

The focus is on **performing technical skills at high speed with maximum efficiency**, simulating the pressure and speed of actual game play.

Intensive technical actions are typically integrated into the training week on the following days for different levels:

- **Professional Microcycle:**
  MD +3/-4 and MD +5/-2 *(see page 19)*
- **Semi-Professional Microcycle:**
  MD +3/-4 *(see page 21)*
- **Youth Academy Microcycle:**
  MD +3/-4 *(see page 22)*
- **Grassroots (Youth) Microcycle:**
  Alternate weeks *(see pages 23-24)*

In this book, we focus on the professional training week. The timing aligns with the microcycle phase methodology, aiming to sharpen players' technical abilities and readiness as the match day approaches.

Intensive technical practices often include **high speed passing combination sequences, receiving skills, and quick dribbling drills**.

NOTE: It is key to maintain a high tempo throughout intensive technical practices, ensuring the players are working at or near their maximum effort levels.

Players engage in **high speed one-touch passing sequences within a confined space, forcing them to think and react quickly**. They receive and pass the ball in quick succession, often from different angles and distances, to mimic match situations.

The practices also often require players to dribble the ball at high speed, using quick footwork and close ball control.

These Intensive Actions:

- **Enhance players' ability to perform under pressure.**
- **Reduce reaction times.**
- **Develop decision making.**
- **Improve overall technical proficiency.**

By using these practices close to match day (MD +5/-2), coaches can ensure that players are at peak readiness, both physically and mentally.

Intensive Technical Practices (Small Spaces)

Intensive Technical Practices within the Training Week (Microcycle)

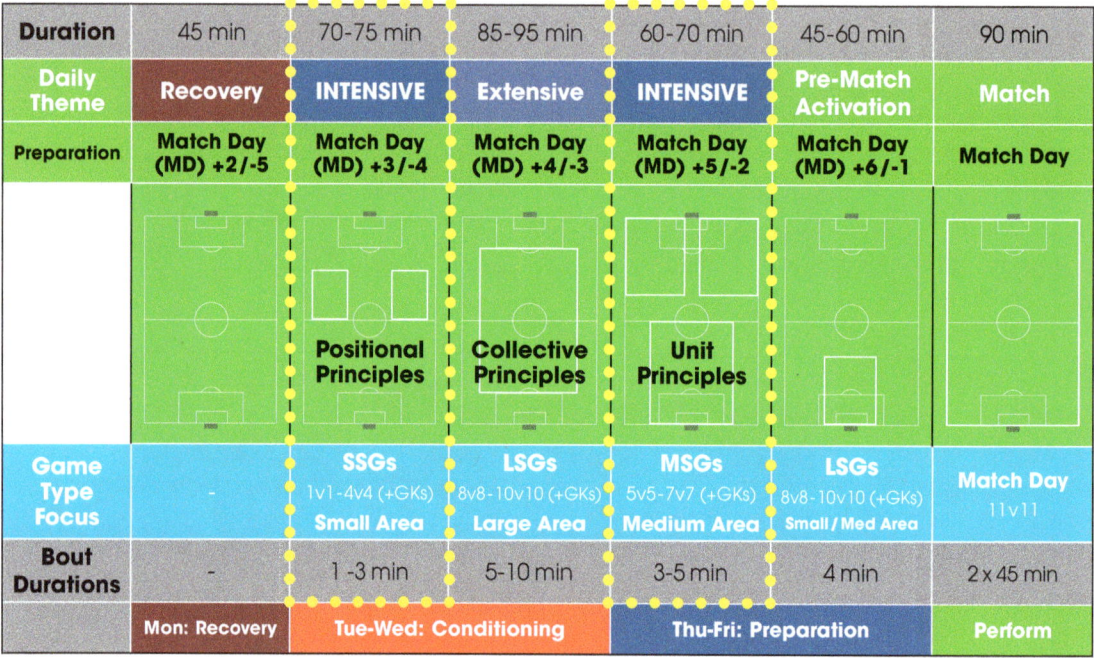

Duration	45 min	70-75 min	85-95 min	60-70 min	45-60 min	90 min
Daily Theme	Recovery	INTENSIVE	Extensive	INTENSIVE	Pre-Match Activation	Match
Preparation	Match Day (MD) +2/-5	Match Day (MD) +3/-4	Match Day (MD) +4/-3	Match Day (MD) +5/-2	Match Day (MD) +6/-1	Match Day
		Positional Principles	Collective Principles	Unit Principles		
Game Type Focus	-	SSGs 1v1-4v4 (+GKs) Small Area	LSGs 8v8-10v10 (+GKs) Large Area	MSGs 5v5-7v7 (+GKs) Medium Area	LSGs 8v8-10v10 (+GKs) Small/Med Area	Match Day 11v11
Bout Durations	-	1-3 min	5-10 min	3-5 min	4 min	2 x 45 min
	Mon: Recovery	Tue-Wed: Conditioning		Thu-Fri: Preparation		Perform

* **Training Week based on Professional Microcycle Example -** see pages 19-20.

- **Intensive Technical Practices** are used on two different training days within the training week.

- **4 Days Until Match (MD +3/-4):**
  Positional Principles Training with Intensive Technical Practices

  * See page 47 for full training session outline.

- **2 Days Until Match (MD +5/-2):**
  Unit Principle Training with Intensive Technical Practices

  * See page 48 for full training session outline.

Intensive Technical Practices (Small Spaces)

Intensive Technical Training Session
4 Days Until Match (MD +3/-4) Example

Positional Principle and Intensive Technical Training Session (70-75 min):

1. Resistance Warm Up (10-12 min)
2. Intensive Technical Practice (10-15 min)
3. Resistance Conditioning Practice (10-20 min)
4. Small Sided Possession (10-12 min)
5. Small Sided Game (10-25 min)

* **Based on Professional Training Week (Microcycle)** - see pages 19-24 for other ages/levels.

Intensive Technical Practices (Small Spaces)

Intensive Technical Training Session
2 Days Until Match (MD +5/-2) Example

Unit Principle and Intensive Technical Training Session (70-75 min):

1. Reaction Speed Warm Up (5-7 min)
2. Intensive Technical Practice (10-15 min)
3. Reaction Speed Conditioning Practice (5-15 min)
4. Medium Sided Possession (6-15 min)
5. Medium Sided Game (10-25 min)

* **Based on Professional Training Week (Microcycle)** - see pages 19-24 for other ages/levels.

Intensive Technical Practices (Small Spaces)

MD +3/-4 and MD +5/-2
Intensive Technical Practices

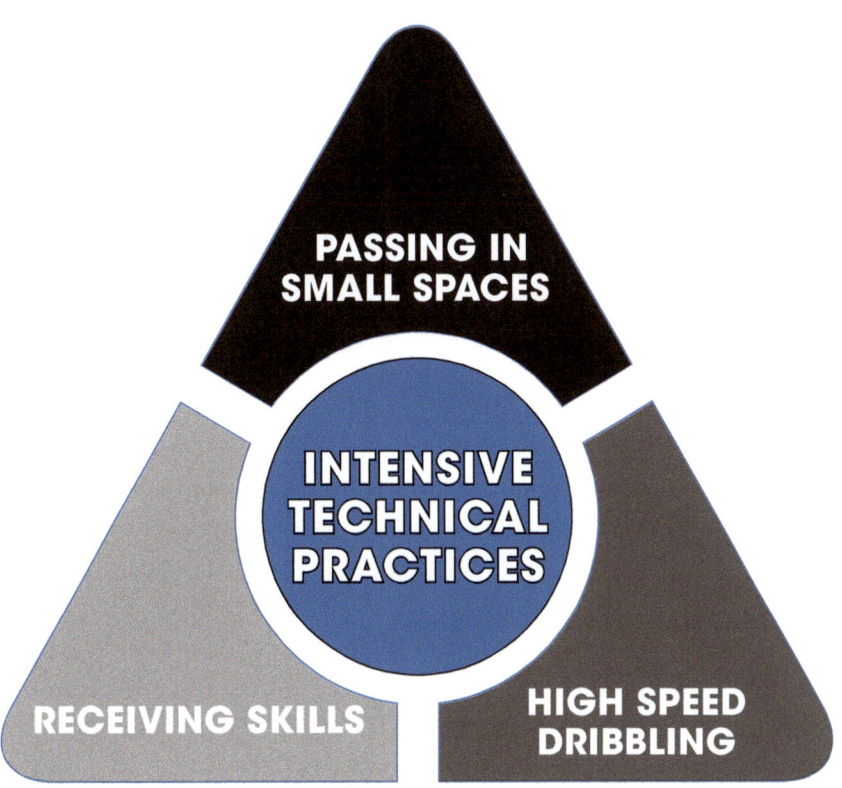

Passing in Small Spaces
High speed one-touch passing combination sequences within small spaces, forcing players to process information quickly and make the best decisions in an instant.

Receiving Skills
A strong emphasis is placed on receiving with the back foot and correct body shape from different angles and distances. The short distances and high pressure prepare the players well for match situations.

High Speed Dribbling
Quick footwork and close ball control.

Why are Intensive Technical Practices Used on MD +3/-4 and MD +5/-2 Days of the Training Week?
Intensive technical practices are used on these training days because they avoid repetitive large distance striking, which reduces the strain on key muscle groups.

How Does this Help to Maximise Performance?
The focus is on managing injury risk and minimising overuse to prevent fatigue while maintaining technical sharpness with quick decision making.

Intensive Technical Practices (Small Spaces)

Key Coaching Points for Intensive Technical Practices (Small Spaces)

Quick Decision Making and Reactions
- Train players to make quick decisions.
- Teach them to adjust their body shape.
- Make sure they can dictate the next passing direction.

Explosive Movements into Passing Lanes
- Dynamic movements to create space with sharp changes of direction.
- Perform explosive sprints to receive or transition to the next phase.
- Maintain balance and control during all movements.

High Ball Speed with Precision
- Emphasise firm and accurate passes.
- Encourage clean ball contacts (firm striking) in tight spaces.
- Focus on precision and control under pressure.

One or Two Touch Passing Under Pressure
- Limit touches to promote quick ball circulation.
- Introduce defensive pressure to create situations similar to matches.
- Use time limits to simulate added pressure.

Intensive Technical Practices (Small Spaces)

1. Juventus Dynamic Speed and Agility Movements Technical Circuit

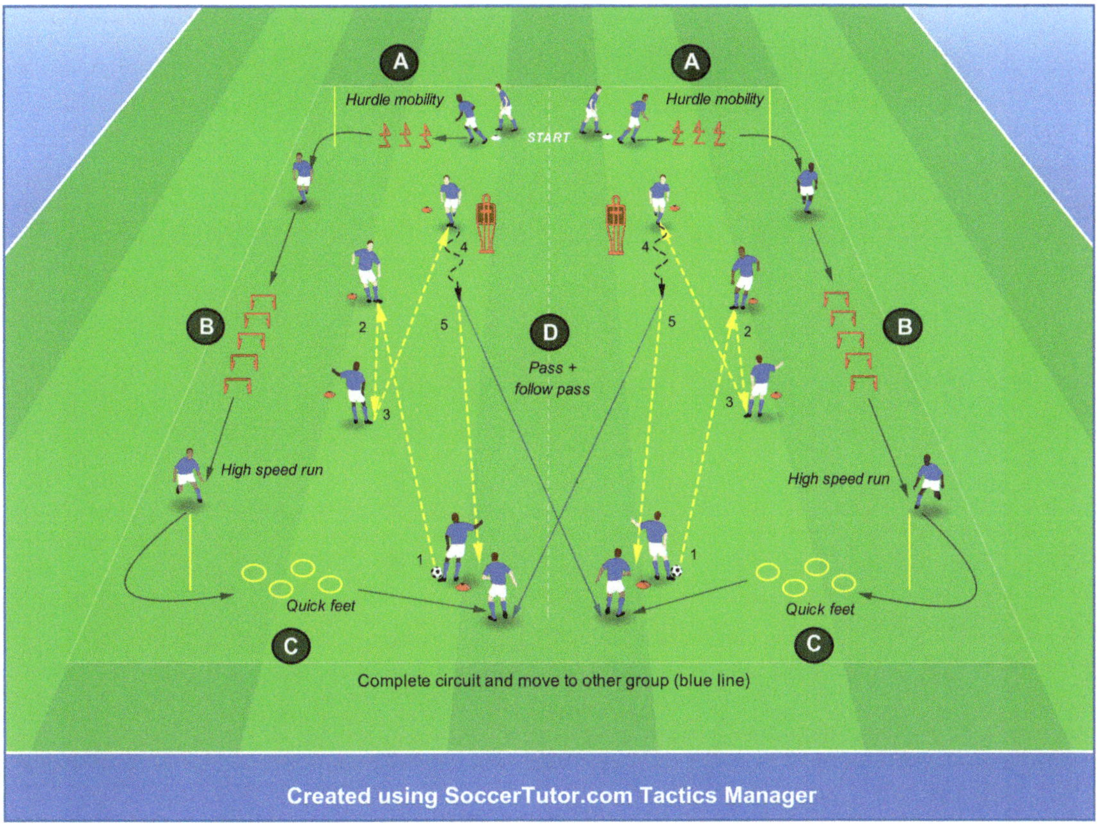

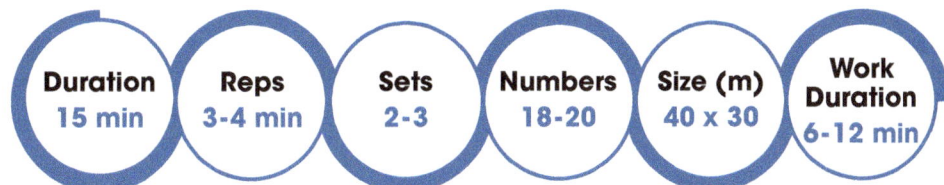

Duration	Reps	Sets	Numbers	Size (m)	Work Duration
15 min	3-4 min	2-3	18-20	40 x 30	6-12 min

OBJECTIVE: Quick feet patterns and dynamic movements through a technical circuit.

- The players start with hurdle mobility through 3 hurdles, then run around the pole to the next 5 hurdles at high speed.

- They perform forward jumps through the 5 hurdles and again run at high speed around the pole. From there, they use quick feet through the speed rings.

- At the next station, there is a 4 player passing combination. All players follow their pass to move around the circuit.

- After receiving, dribbling past the mannequin, and passing to the next player waiting at the start, the players move across to the opposite group.

Intensive Technical Practices (Small Spaces)

2. Real Madrid "In and Out" Dribbling and Passing Circuit

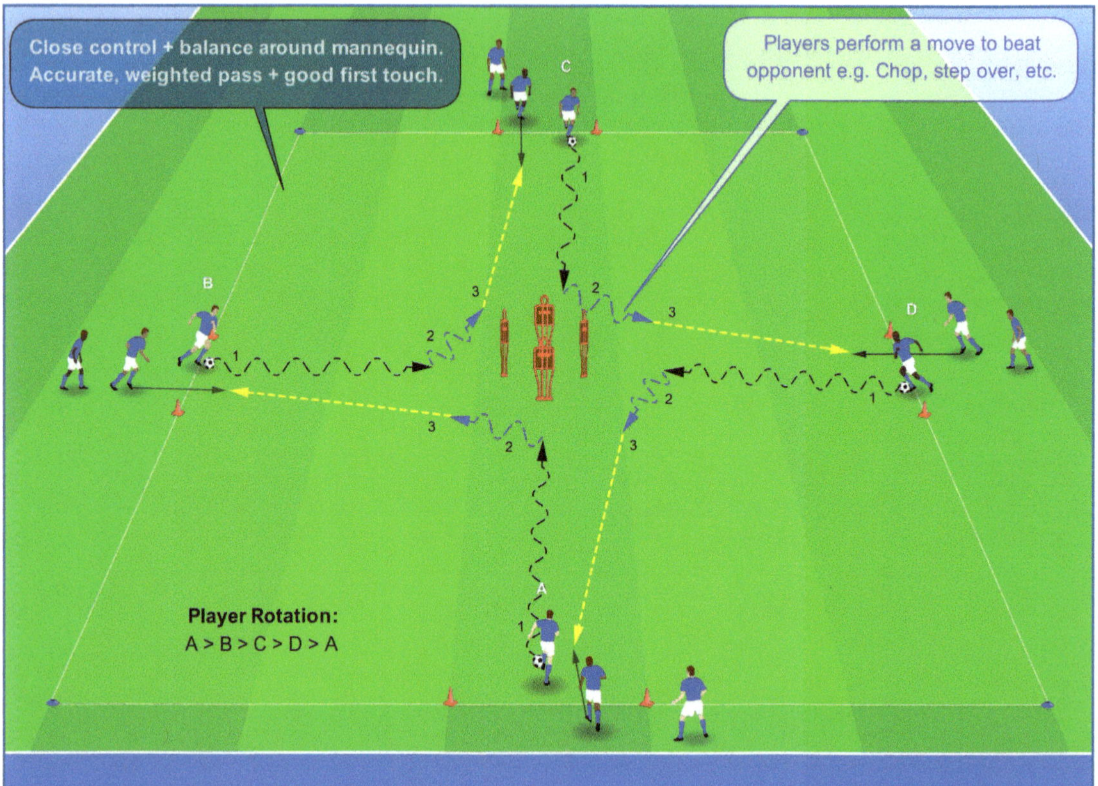

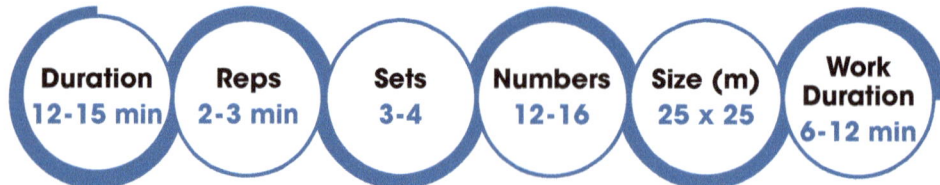

Created using SoccerTutor.com Tactics Manager

Duration	Reps	Sets	Numbers	Size (m)	Work Duration
12-15 min	2-3 min	3-4	12-16	25 x 25	6-12 min

OBJECTIVE: High speed passing, first touch, and ability to dribble past an opponent.

- There are 4 mannequins in the centre and 3 players behind each cone gate.
- To start, one player from each group dribbles the ball into the centre and performs a skill (e.g. chop, step over, etc) to the left of the mannequin.
- After performing the skill, they pass to the next player waiting in the next group: A → B → C → D → A.
- Once all players have completed 3 full circuits, the coach changes the skill.
- **Progression:** Make it a race and the players compete to see who can complete a full circuit the quickest.

©SOCCERTUTOR.COM

Technical to Maximise Performance

Intensive Technical Practices (Small Spaces)

3. Technical Receiving (Body Shape) Rotational Passing Combinations

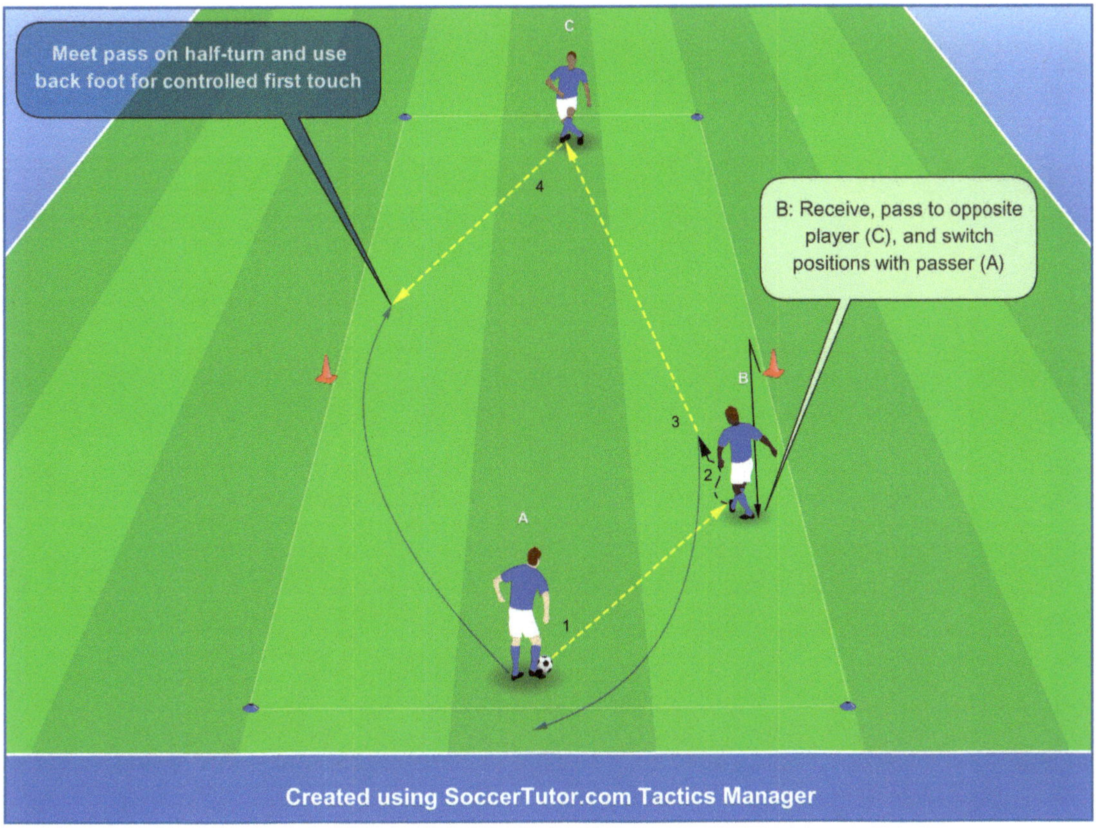

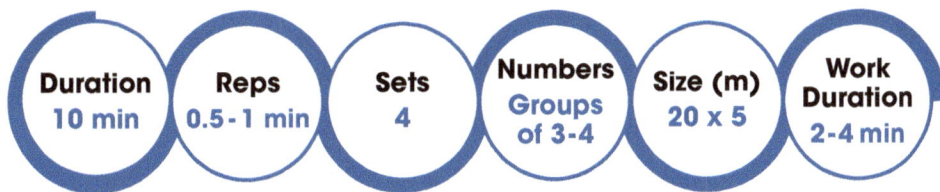

Duration	Reps	Sets	Numbers	Size (m)	Work Duration
10 min	0.5 - 1 min	4	Groups of 3-4	20 x 5	2 - 4 min

OBJECTIVE: Explosive actions between passes, constant rotations, body shape to play.

- Set up with 2-3 players at the ends and 1 player in the middle.
- **A** passes to the middle player (**B**), who receives on the half-turn, and passes to the opposite end player (**C**). **A** and **B** switch positions. **C** passes to **A** (new middle player) as the practice continues.

- **Coaching Points:** Focus on technique, quality of the pass, and quick movements after passing.
- **Timings:** The players rest every 30 seconds to one minute. Break up the practice with some dynamic flexibility work between repetitions.

Intensive Technical Practices (Small Spaces)

4. Bayern Munich Open Up to Receive Play Through and Around Passing

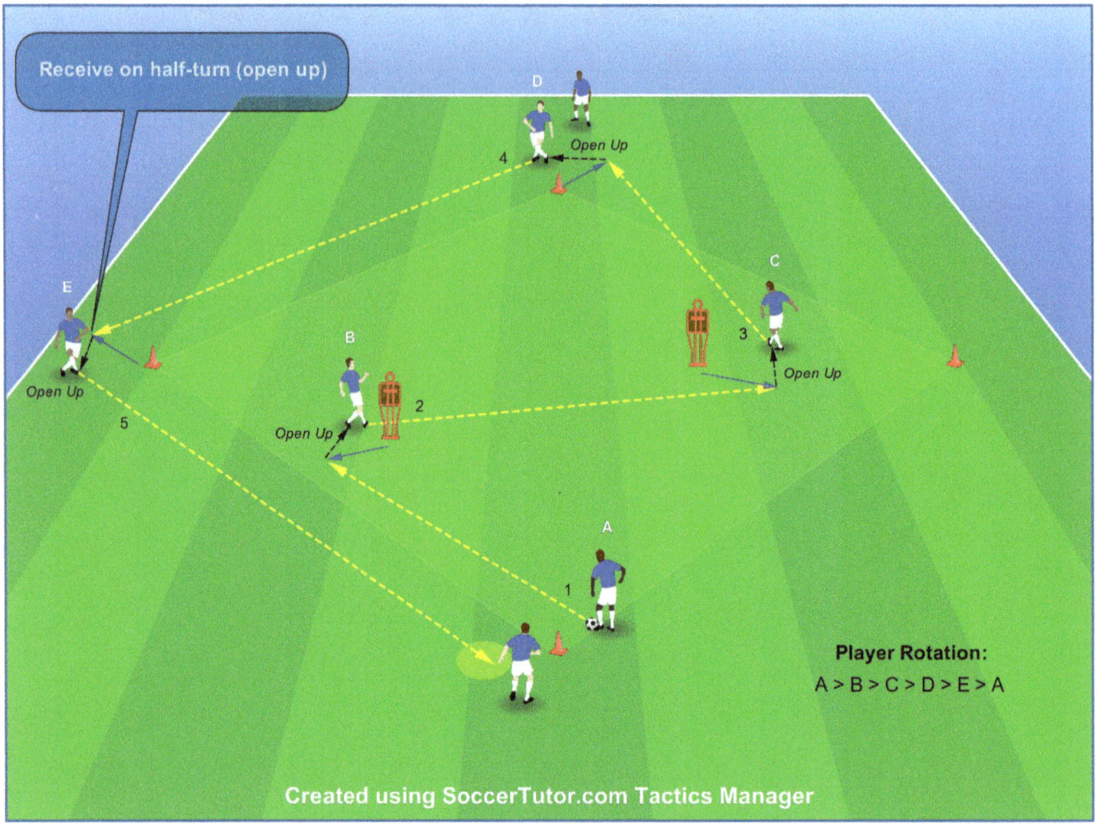

[Diagram: Receive on half-turn (open up). Players A, B, C, D, E positioned in a 20x20 area with mannequins and cones. Passing sequence 1–5. Player Rotation: A > B > C > D > E > A]

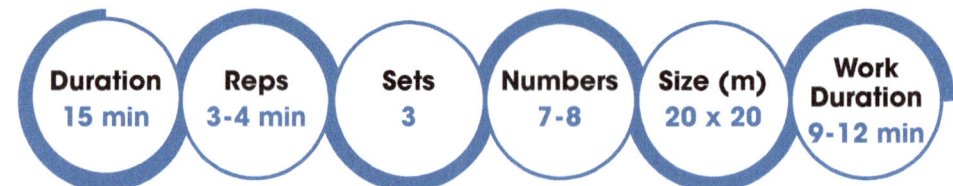

Duration	Reps	Sets	Numbers	Size (m)	Work Duration
15 min	3-4 min	3	7-8	20 x 20	9-12 min

OBJECTIVE: Back foot receiving, pass placement, and body shape to receive.

- **A** passes diagonally to **B**, who opens up to receive around the mannequin.
- **B** passes across to **C**, who also opens up to receive around the mannequin.
- **C** passes forward to **D**, who opens up to receive around the cone, and passes to **E**, who does the same.
- **E** passes to Position A and the next player waiting continues the same sequence. All players follow their pass.
- **Coaching Points:** Quality and weight of pass, receive on the half-turn, quick combination play, good movement to receive, and intensity of play/rotations.

Intensive Technical Practices (Small Spaces)

5. Technical Receiving and Support Play Passing Combinations

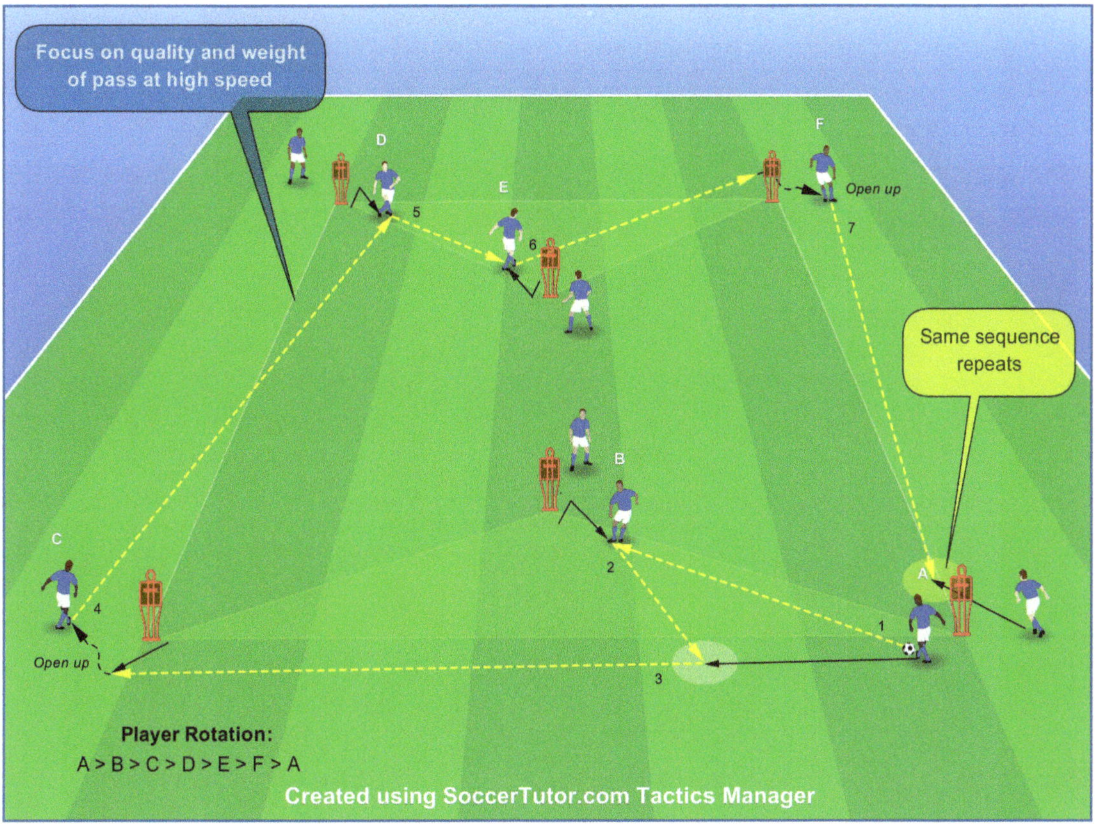

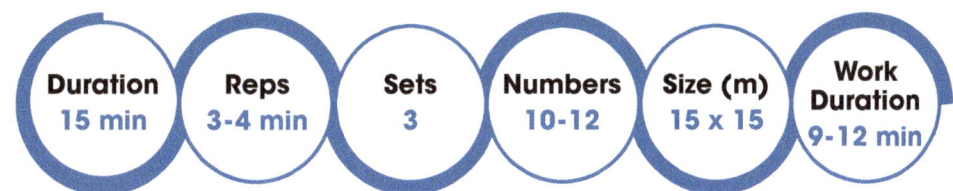

Duration	Reps	Sets	Numbers	Size (m)	Work Duration
15 min	3-4 min	3	10-12	15 x 15	9-12 min

OBJECTIVE: Passing combinations, movements, support play, and body shape.

- **A** passes to **B** and moves to receive the return (one-two).
- **A** passes to **C**, who opens up to receive around the mannequin, and then plays a firm ground pass to **D**.
- **D** passes to **E**, **E** to **F**, and finally **F** to Position A for the next player waiting.
- All players rotate and follow their pass as the practice continues.
- **Coaching Points:** Quality and weight of pass, quick combination play, good movement to receive, opening up to receive on back foot, and intensity of play/rotations.

Technical to Maximise Performance

Intensive Technical Practices (Small Spaces)

6. Up, Back, and Through Passing and Switching Play Combination

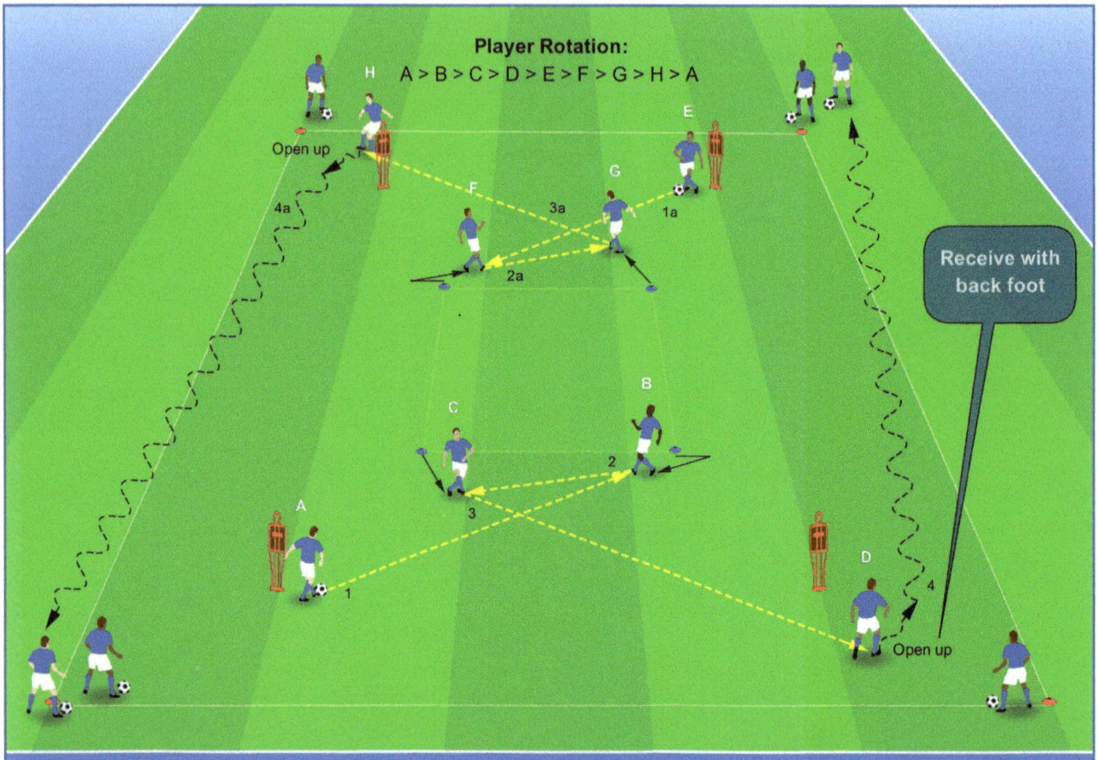

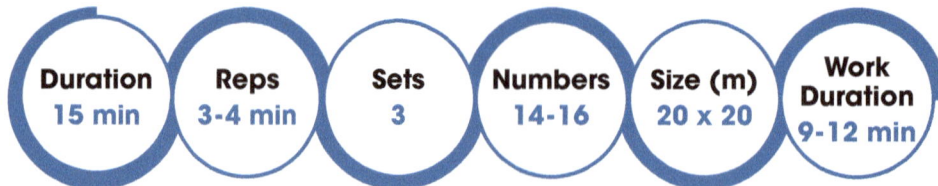

Duration	Reps	Sets	Numbers	Size (m)	Work Duration
15 min	3-4 min	3	14-16	20 x 20	9-12 min

OBJECTIVE: Combination play passing (up, back, and through) and switches of play.

- In groups of 14-16 players, two balls start simultaneously from players **A** and **E**.
- **A/E** pass diagonally to **B/F**, who set the ball for **C/G** to switch the play to **D/H**.
- **D/H** must receive the ball behind the mannequin (open up) and take a good directional first touch out of their feet.
- To complete the sequence, **D/H** dribble the ball to Position A/E.
- As soon as **D/H** take the ball around the mannequin, the two next players waiting both pass a new ball in to continue.
- The players rotate their positions by following their pass, as shown.

Technical to Maximise Performance

Intensive Technical Practices (Small Spaces)

7. End to End Third Man Run Combinations to Play Forward

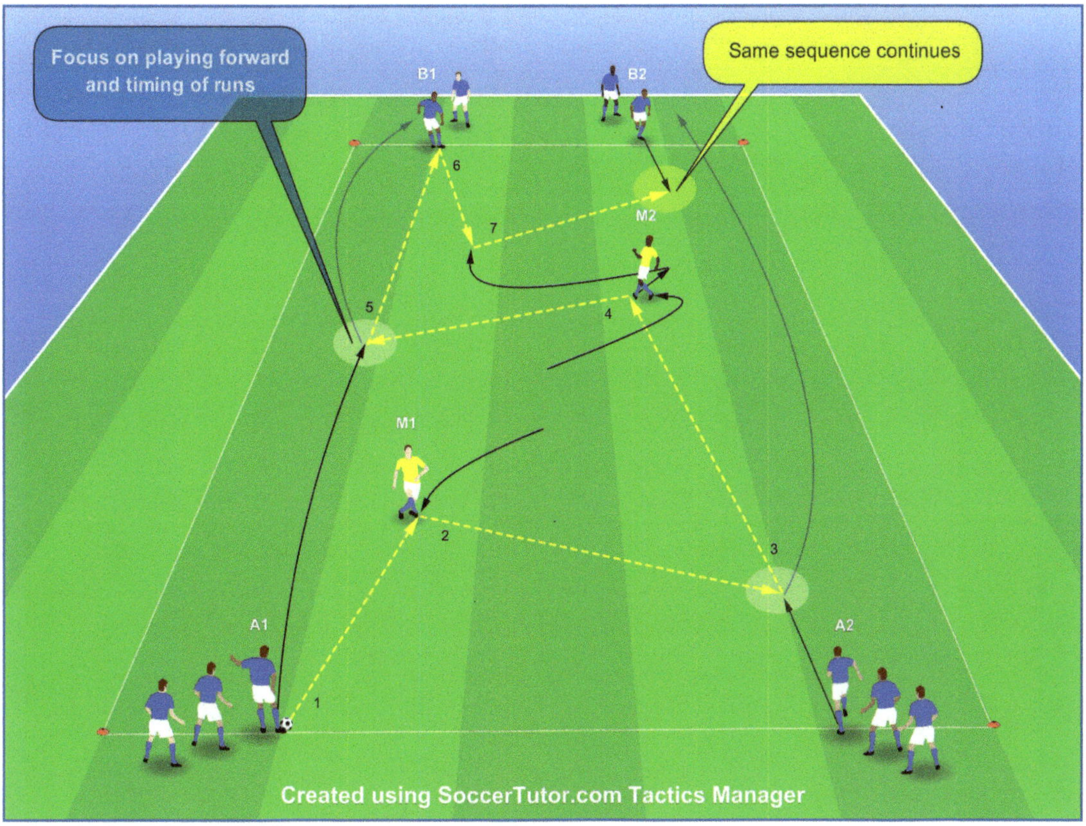

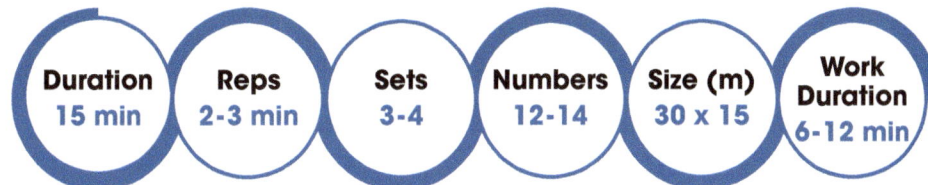

Duration	Reps	Sets	Numbers	Size (m)	Work Duration
15 min	2-3 min	3-4	12-14	30 x 15	6-12 min

OBJECTIVE: Combination play passing, timing of runs, and focus on playing forward.

- In groups of 12-14, the players are in pairs at the ends except for the 2 central area players (**M1** and **M2**).

- **A1** passes to **M1**, who sets the ball for **A2** to play forward to **M2**.

- **M2** then sets the ball for the oncoming run of **A1** to pass to the end player **B1**.

- Both **A1** and **A2** run to the opposite end and the next pair continues (**B1** and **B2**) in the opposite direction, supported by **M1** and **M2**.

- **Note:** The same pattern continues until the coach changes the combination sequence.

©SOCCERTUTOR.COM   Technical to Maximise Performance

Intensive Technical Practices (Small Spaces)

8. Ajax Triangle Open Up to Receive Rotational Passing

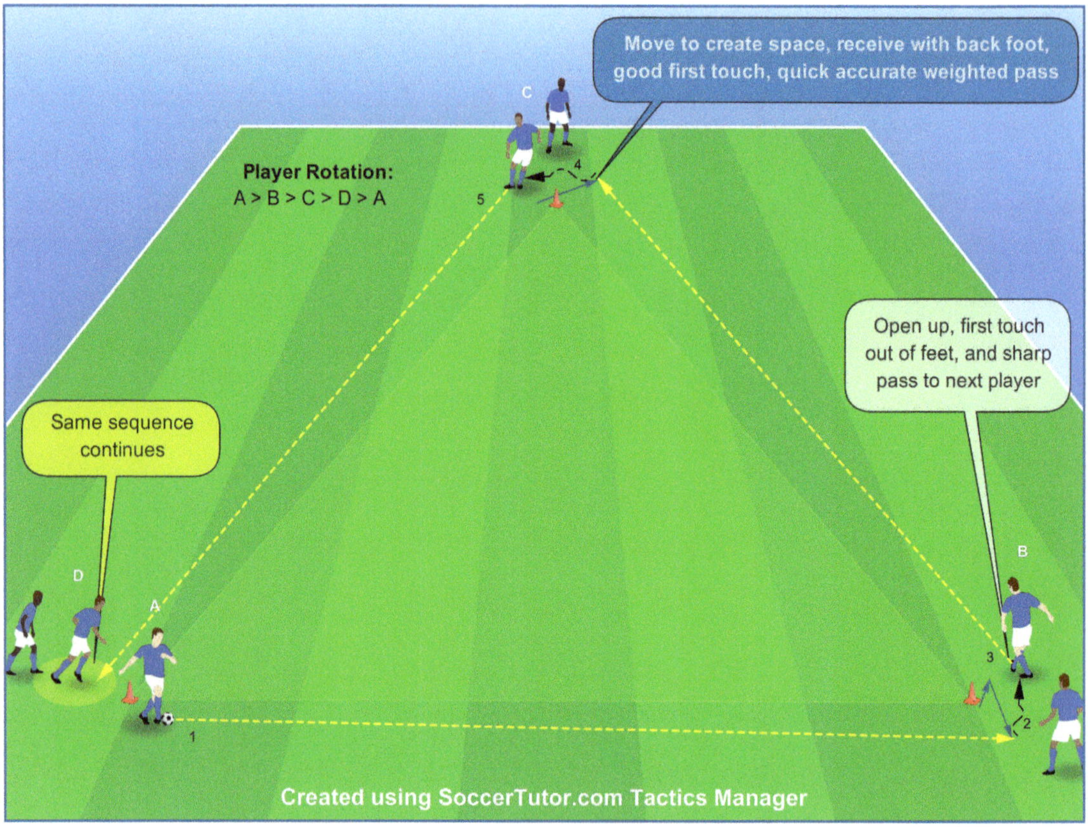

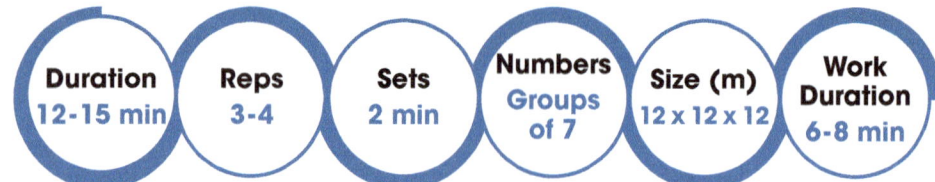

OBJECTIVE: Movement, back foot receiving, first touch, and quick accurate passing.

- The players work in groups of 7 for this first variation of the Ajax Triangle.
- Each receiving player must check away from the cone before moving to receive.
- From there, they then open up, and take their first touch out of their feet and around the cone.
- They then deliver a sharp pass to the next player (**A → B → C → D → A**) in the rotation and the sequence continues.

©SOCCERTUTOR.COM

Technical to Maximise Performance

Intensive Technical Practices (Small Spaces)

9. Ajax Triangle Rotational Passing with One-Two Support Play

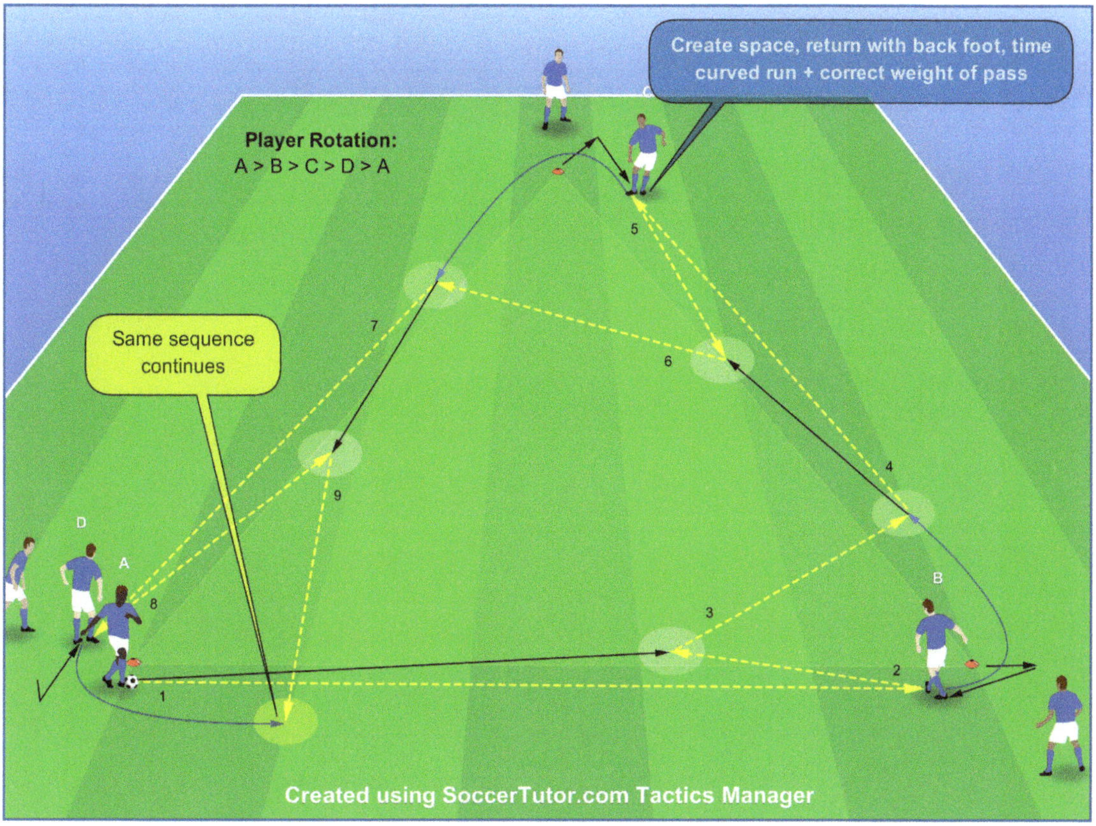

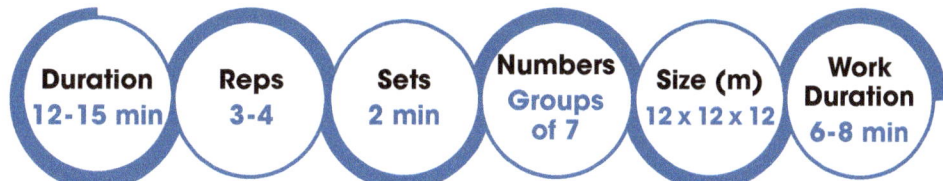

Duration	Reps	Sets	Numbers	Size (m)	Work Duration
12-15 min	3-4	2 min	Groups of 7	12 x 12 x 12	6-8 min

OBJECTIVE: Movement, body shape, back foot receiving, and quick accurate passing.

- This is a progression of the previous practice and a second of 4 variations of the Ajax triangle.
- **A** passes to **B** and moves towards them in support.
- There is then a one-two played in each corner as the ball rotates around.
- The players move around the cone to receive the return pass before playing to the next player.
- **Coaching Point:** Players must take care when setting the pass (correct weight) in front of the cone for their teammate to pass to the next player.

Technical to Maximise Performance

Intensive Technical Practices (Small Spaces)

10. Ajax Triangle One-Two Support and Quick Combination Play

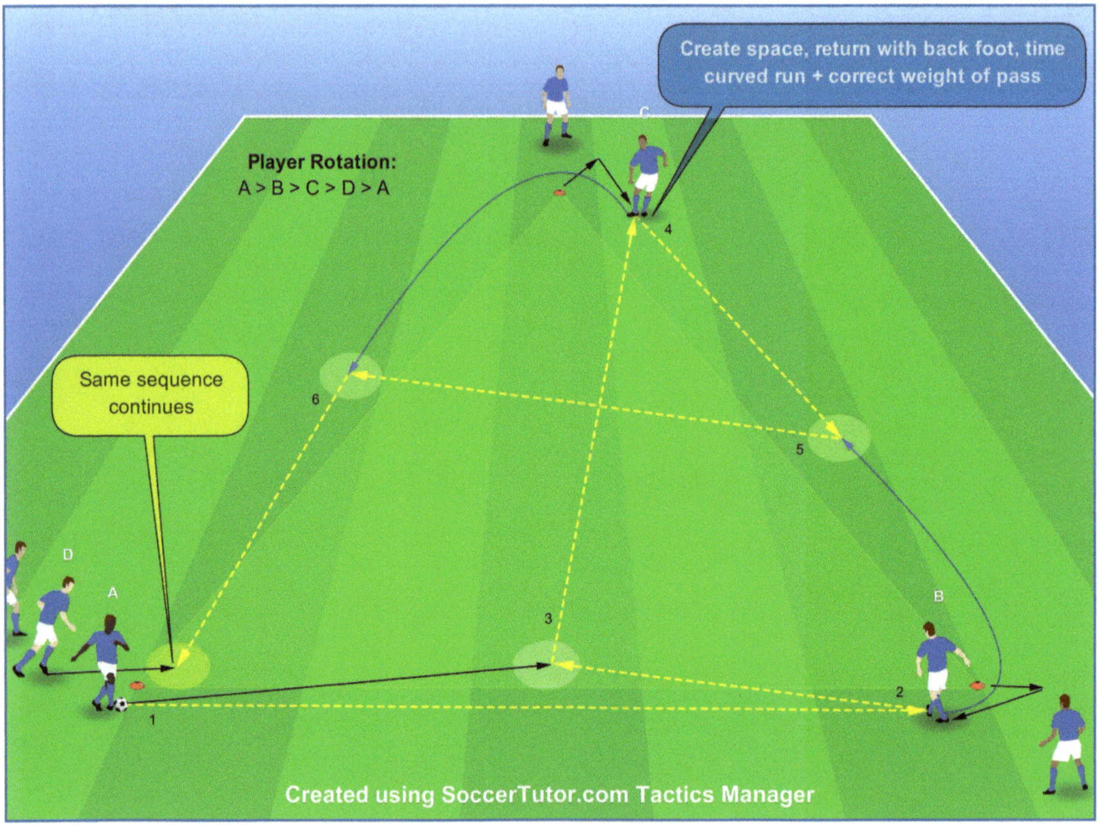

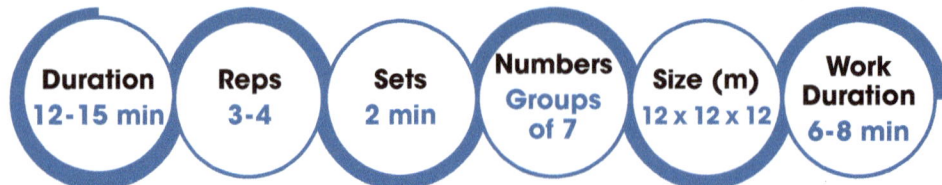

Duration	Reps	Sets	Numbers	Size (m)	Work Duration
12-15 min	3-4	2 min	Groups of 7	12 x 12 x 12	6-8 min

OBJECTIVE: Movement, body shape, back foot receiving, and quick accurate passing.

- This is the third of 4 variations of the Ajax triangle.
- **A** passes to **B** and moves towards them in support. **A** passes forward to **C**, who sets the ball back for **B** to move onto.
- **B** passes across for the run of **C** around the cone. **C** passes to **D**, who continues.
- **Note: B** and **C** check away from the cone before moving to receive their first pass.
- **Coaching Point:** Players must take care when setting the pass (correct weight) in front of the cone for their teammate to pass to the next player.

©SOCCERTUTOR.COM — Technical to Maximise Performance

Intensive Technical Practices (Small Spaces)

11. Ajax Triangle Free Player Decision Making Passing Combinations

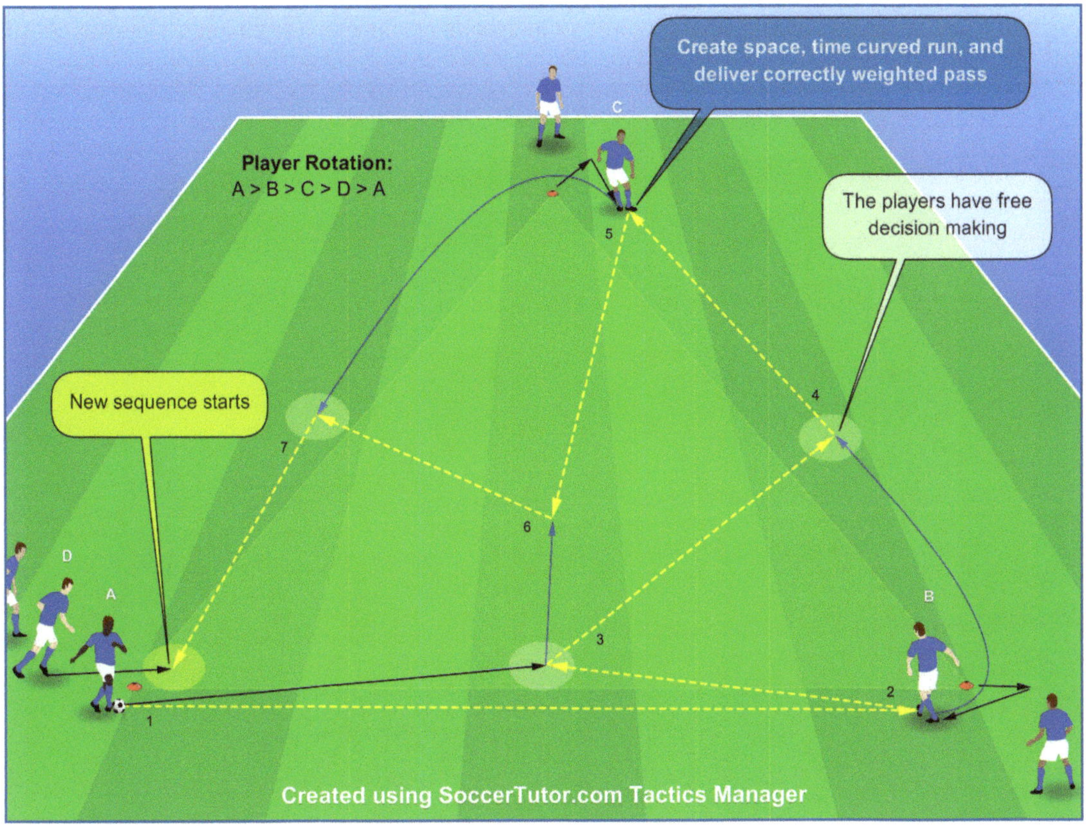

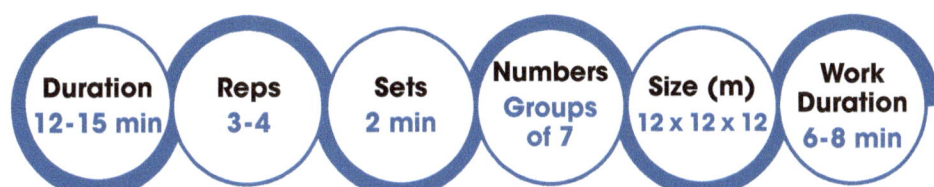

Duration	Reps	Sets	Numbers	Size (m)	Work Duration
12-15 min	3-4	2 min	Groups of 7	12 x 12 x 12	6-8 min

OBJECTIVE: Movement, body shape, back foot receiving, and quick accurate passing.

- This is a progression of the previous practice and the fourth and final variation of the Ajax triangle.
- Players now make their own decisions.
- They can pass around the triangle with different combinations and in different directions of their choosing.
- They must still always follow the same rotation: A → B → C → D → A.
- The diagram shows one example.
- **Coaching Point:** Players must take care when setting the pass (correct weight) in front of the cone for their teammate to pass to the next player.

Intensive Technical Practices (Small Spaces)

12. Aerial Passing and Receiving Technical Triangle

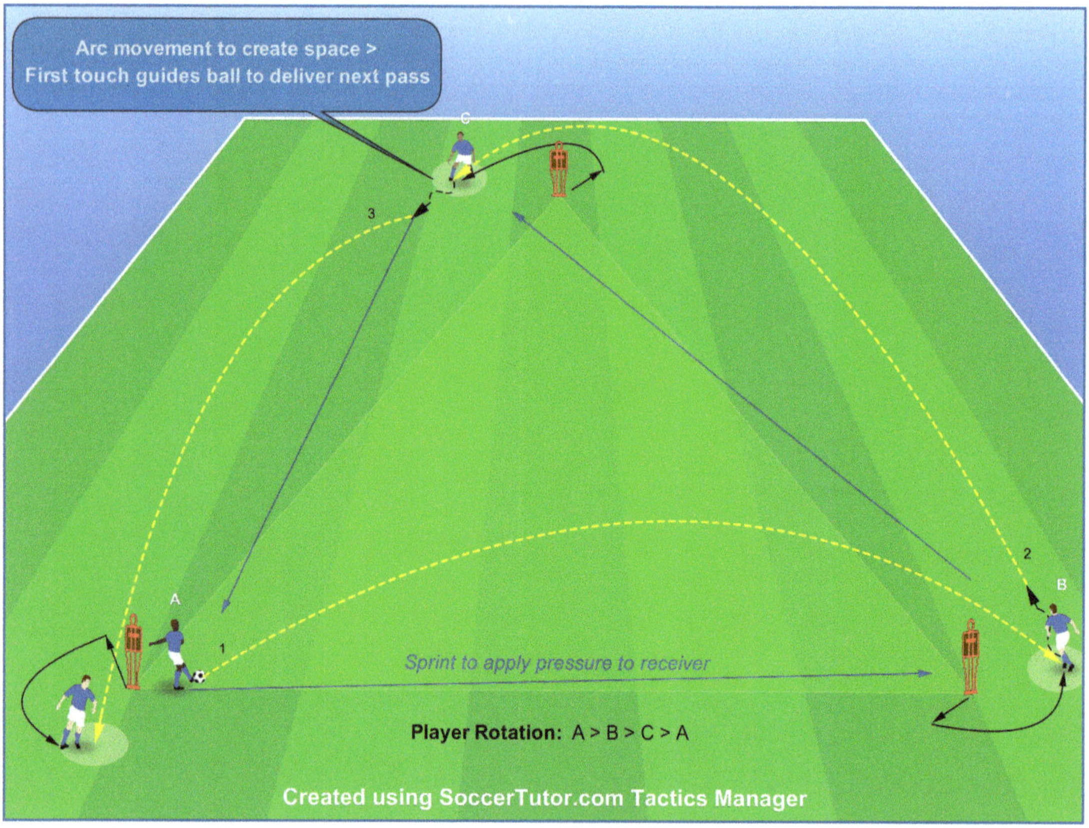

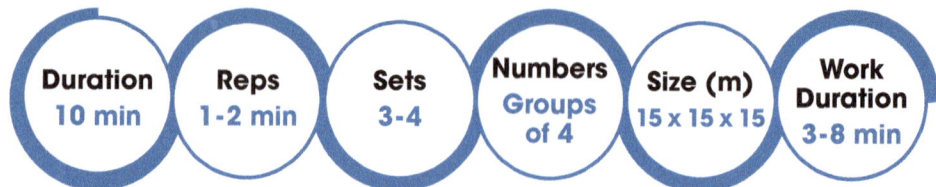

OBJECTIVE: High speed aerial passing and body shape (back foot) to receive.

- **A** starts by playing an aerial pass over the mannequin to **B**, who checks off the mannequin, receives with good body shape (back foot), and then plays an aerial pass for **C**.
- **C** does the same for the next player at Position A in this continuous sequence.

- After each pass, players sprint to the next station (blue arrows), adding pressure to the receiver.
- **Coaching Points:** Focus on ball striking (different parts of foot), passing accuracy, and good directional first touches to best set up the next pass.

Intensive Technical Practices (Small Spaces)

13. High Speed Triangle Combination Play with Angled Passing

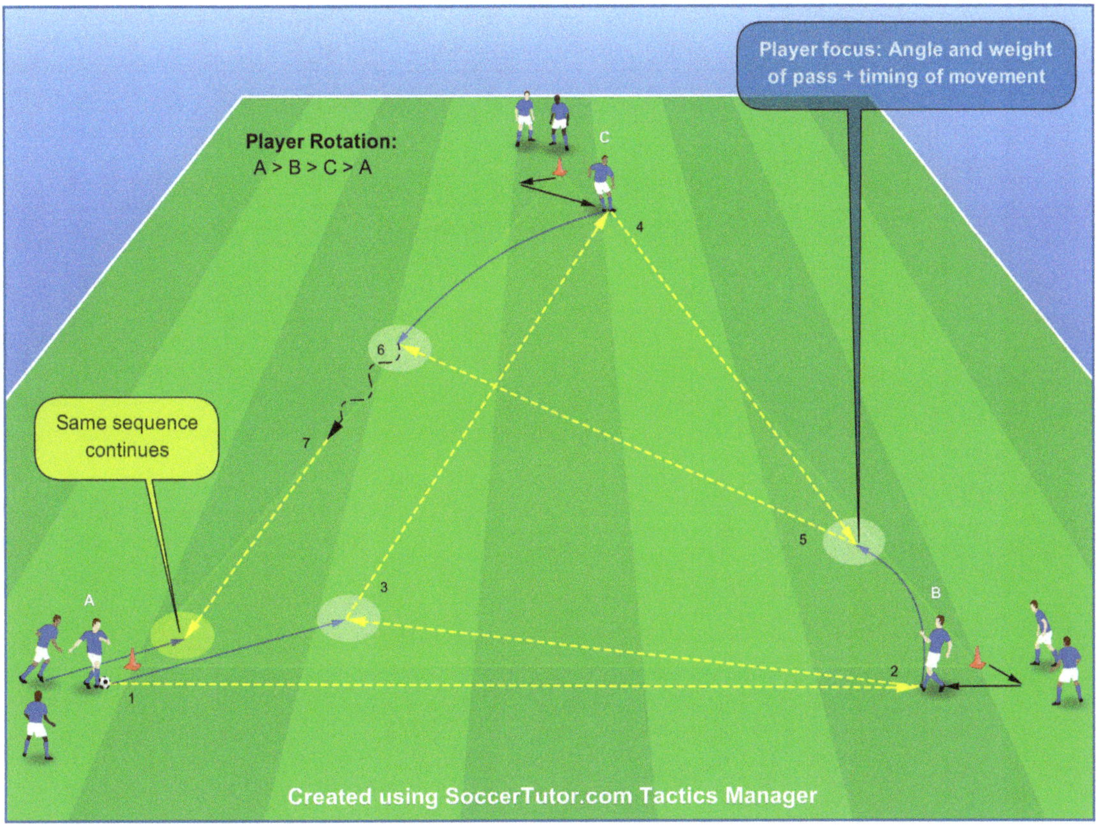

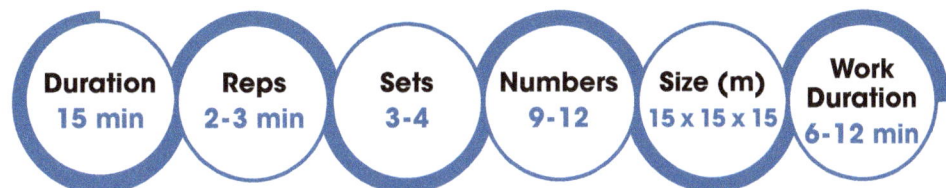

Duration	Reps	Sets	Numbers	Size (m)	Work Duration
15 min	2-3 min	3-4	9-12	15 x 15 x 15	6-12 min

OBJECTIVE: Speed, angle of pass, direction, timing of movement, and ball control.

- **Simple Starting Sequence:**
  A passes to **B**, who then passes to **C**. **C** dribbles to the start (**A**).

- **Progression (Diagram Example):**
  A passes to **B**, who passes back for the movement of **A** (one-two). **A** then passes forward to **C**, who sets the ball back for the oncoming **B**.

- **B** passes across for **C** to run onto (completing the one-two).

- **C** receives, dribbles the ball for a few steps, and then passes to the next player waiting at the start (<u>Position A</u>).

- The same sequence continues.

Technical to Maximise Performance

Intensive Technical Practices (Small Spaces)

14. Up, Back, and Through with Give & Go Passing "Y" (Speed and Timing)

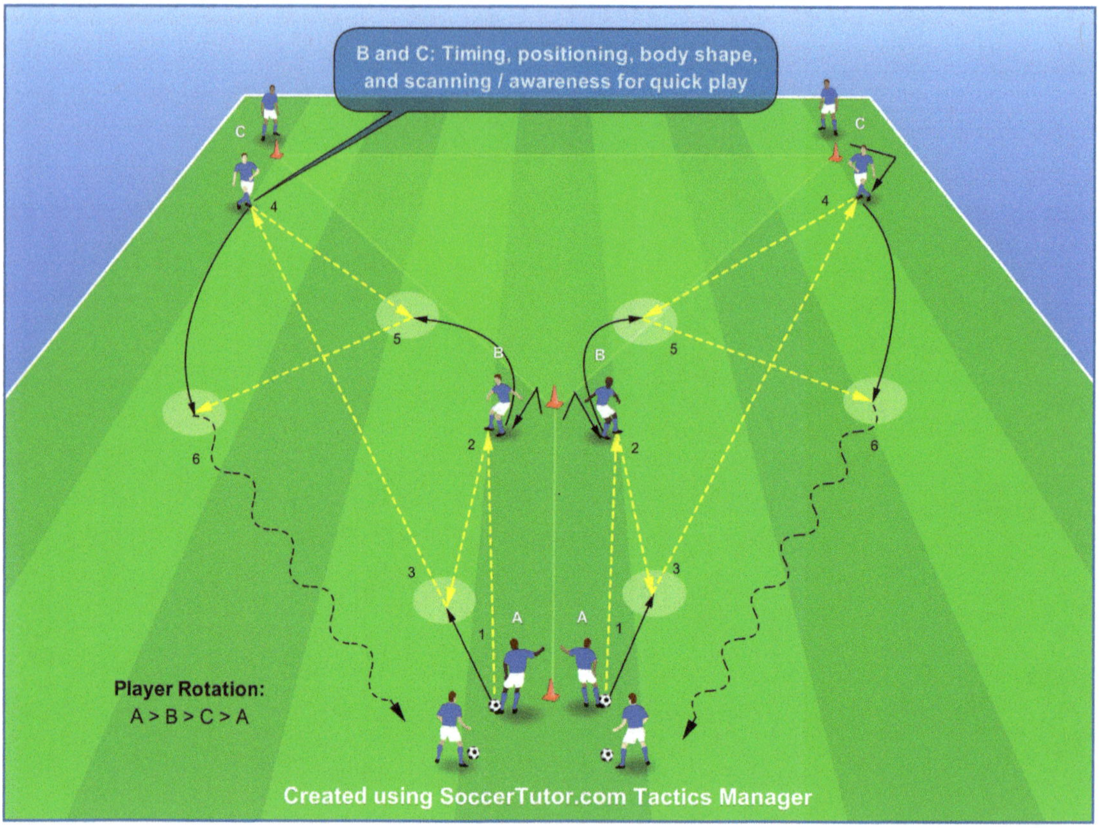

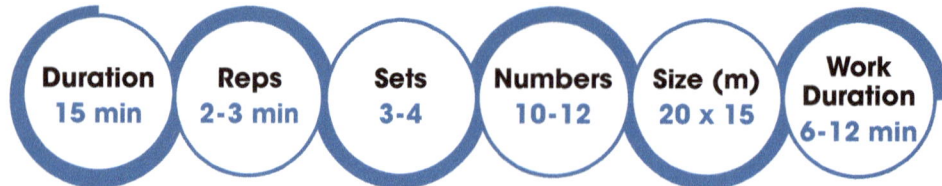

Duration	Reps	Sets	Numbers	Size (m)	Work Duration
15 min	2-3 min	3-4	10-12	20 x 15	6-12 min

OBJECTIVE: Speed, direction, angle of pass, timing of movement, and ball control.

- Play with 2 balls (both sides).
- **A** plays a one-two with **B**, who checks off the cone to receive. **A** then passes diagonally forward to **C**.
- **C** sets the ball for the oncoming **B**, who then passes for **C** to run onto and dribble to the start.
- The sequence is then repeated with the next player waiting.
- **Coaching Point:** For the combination between **B** and **C**, the emphasis is on timing, positioning, and awareness.

Intensive Technical Practices (Small Spaces)

15. Up, Back, Through, and Around Passing "Y" with Angled Forward Passing

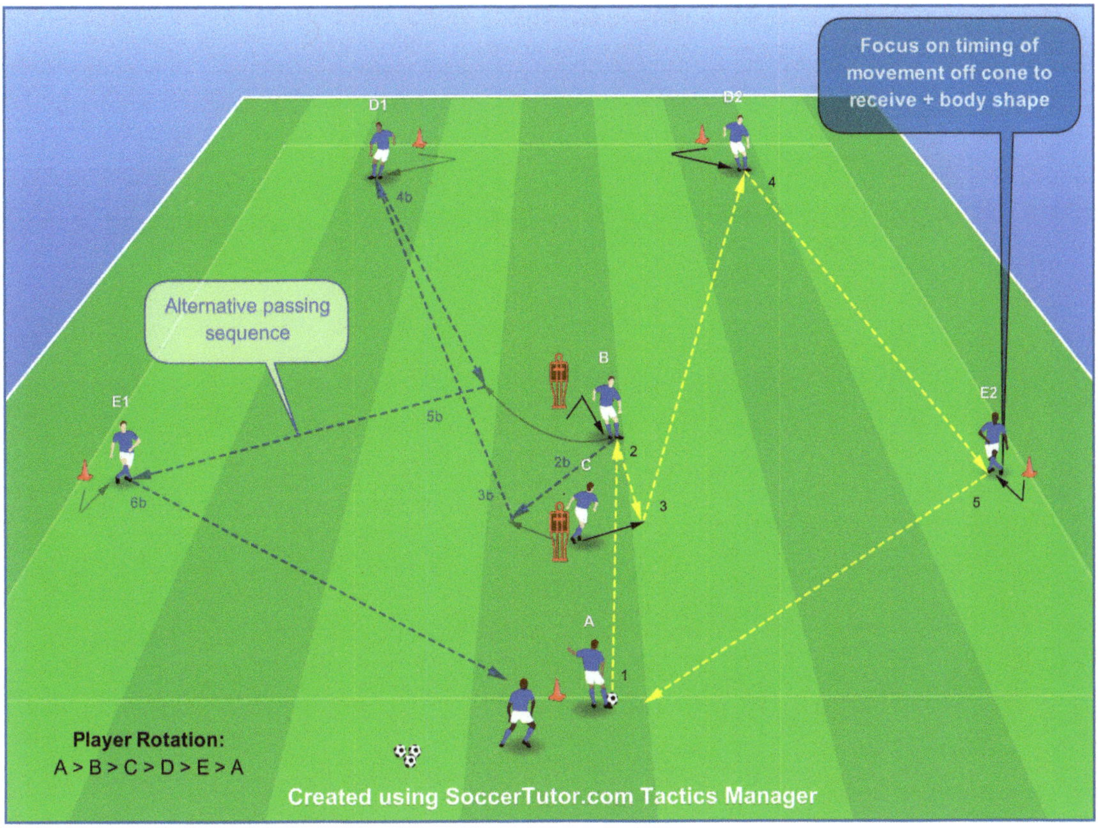

[Diagram: Training setup showing players A, B, C, D1, D2, E1, E2 with passing sequences. Notes include "Focus on timing of movement off cone to receive + body shape" and "Alternative passing sequence". Player Rotation: A > B > C > D > E > A]

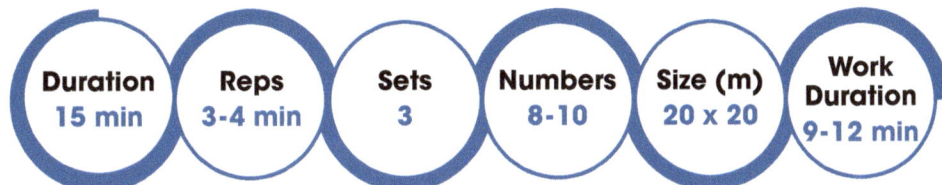

OBJECTIVE: Quality of pass, rotations, receive on half-turn, and angled forward passing.

- **A** passes to **B**, who checks off the cone before moving to receive, then sets the ball back for **C**.
- **C** passes diagonally forward to **D2**.
- **D2** also checks off the cone before moving to receive and passes diagonally back to **E2**.
- **E2** passes to the start for the next player waiting. The practice continues on the left side and an example pattern is shown with the blue arrows.
- **Coaching Points:** Ball speed, timing of movement off the cone and to receive, body shape, and receiving on back foot.

Intensive Technical Practices (Small Spaces)

16. Passing Combination Play and Dribbling Technical Skills "Y" Passing Race

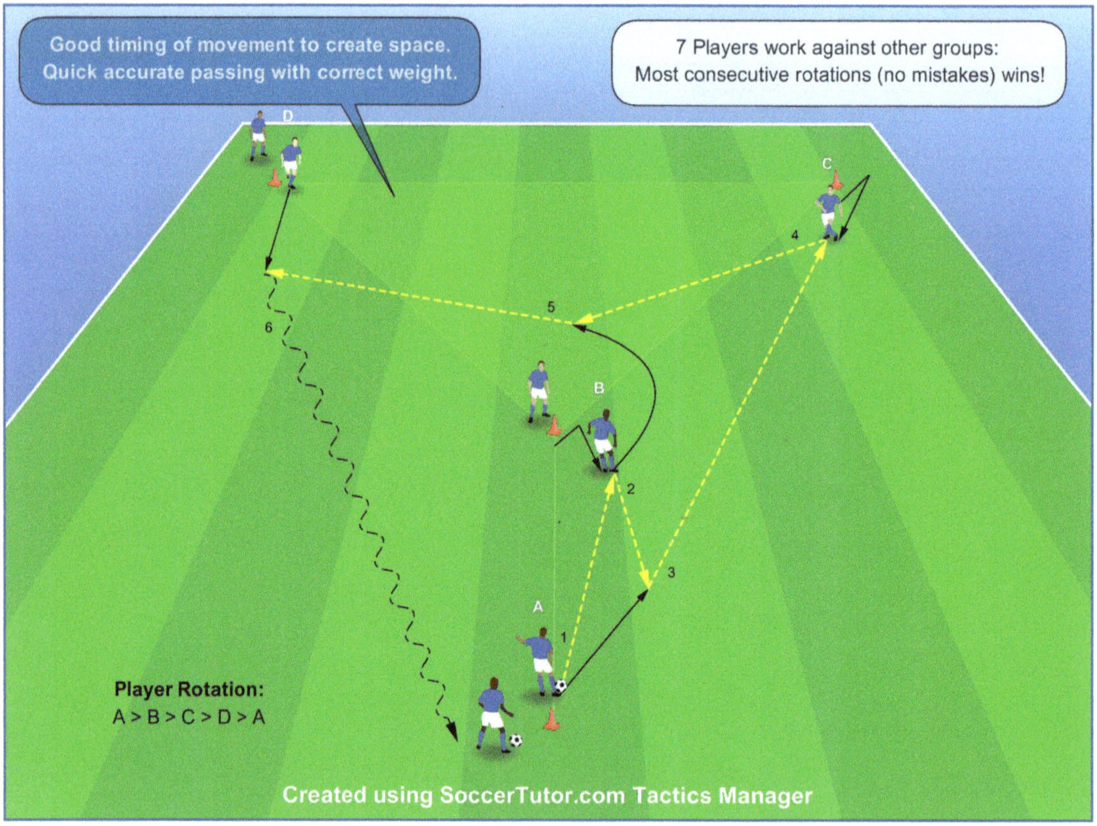

Good timing of movement to create space. Quick accurate passing with correct weight.

7 Players work against other groups: Most consecutive rotations (no mistakes) wins!

Player Rotation:
A > B > C > D > A

Created using SoccerTutor.com Tactics Manager

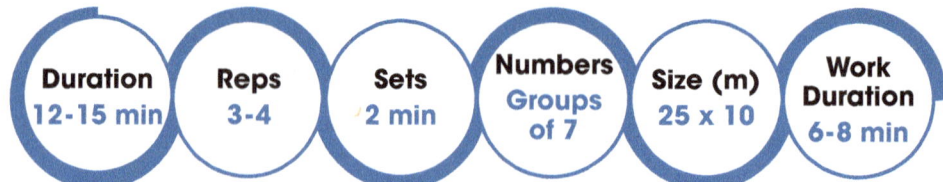

Duration	Reps	Sets	Numbers	Size (m)	Work Duration
12-15 min	3-4	2 min	Groups of 7	25 x 10	6-8 min

OBJECTIVE: Receiving on back foot, body shape, accurate passing, and dribbling.

- Players work in groups of 7 and compete against other groups. The team that completes the most consecutive rotations within a set time wins. If there is a mistake, the count restarts from zero. The coach can change the combination sequence after each competition (set).

- In this example, **A** plays a one-two with **B**, and then passes to **C**.

- **B** then moves forward to receive the next pass from **C** and passes across for **D** to run onto and dribble to Position A.

- The next player goes and the sequence repeats.

Intensive Technical Practices (Small Spaces)

17. Create Space to Lose a Defender and Scanning Double Movement Diamond Passing

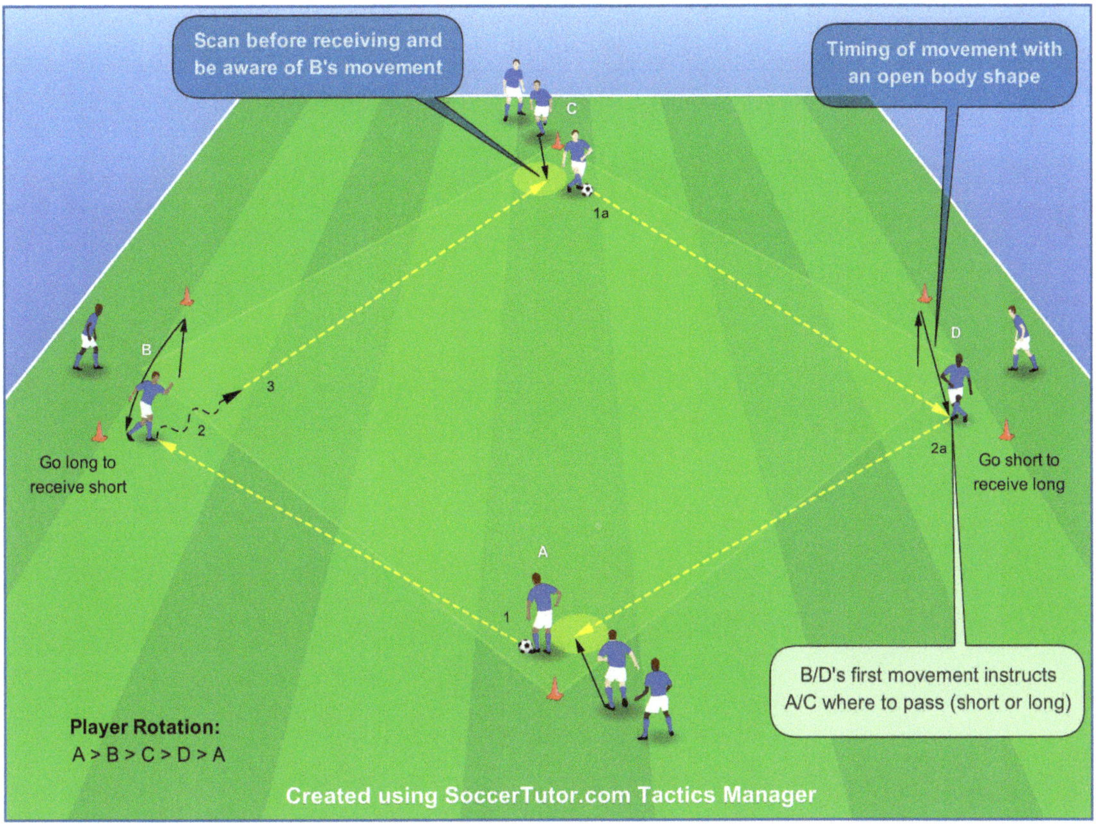

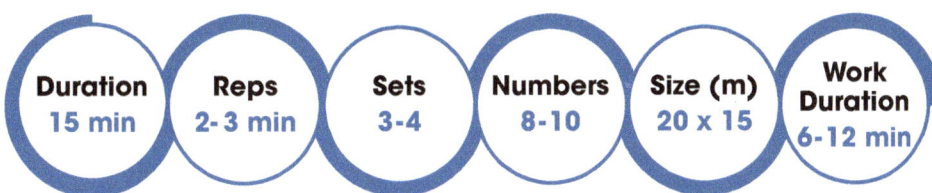

OBJECTIVE: First/second movements, timing, body shape, and scanning.

- This diamond passing circuit starts with 2 balls simultaneously from **A** and **C**.

- The sequence is simple (**A -> B → C → D**) but the type of pass from **A** and **C** varies.

- **B/D** make first movements either short or long, which then determines whether **A/C** pass short or long.

- **B/D** either move long to receive short and turn (**B** in diagram) or move short to receive long and then play a first time pass (**D** in diagram).

- **Progression:** Add overlaps and set backs to the combination sequence, always emphasising scanning and awareness.

Duration	Reps	Sets	Numbers	Size (m)	Work Duration
15 min	2-3 min	3-4	8-10	20 x 15	6-12 min

Intensive Technical Practices (Small Spaces)

18. Pass and Make Opposite Movement "Cross Shape" Diamond Passing

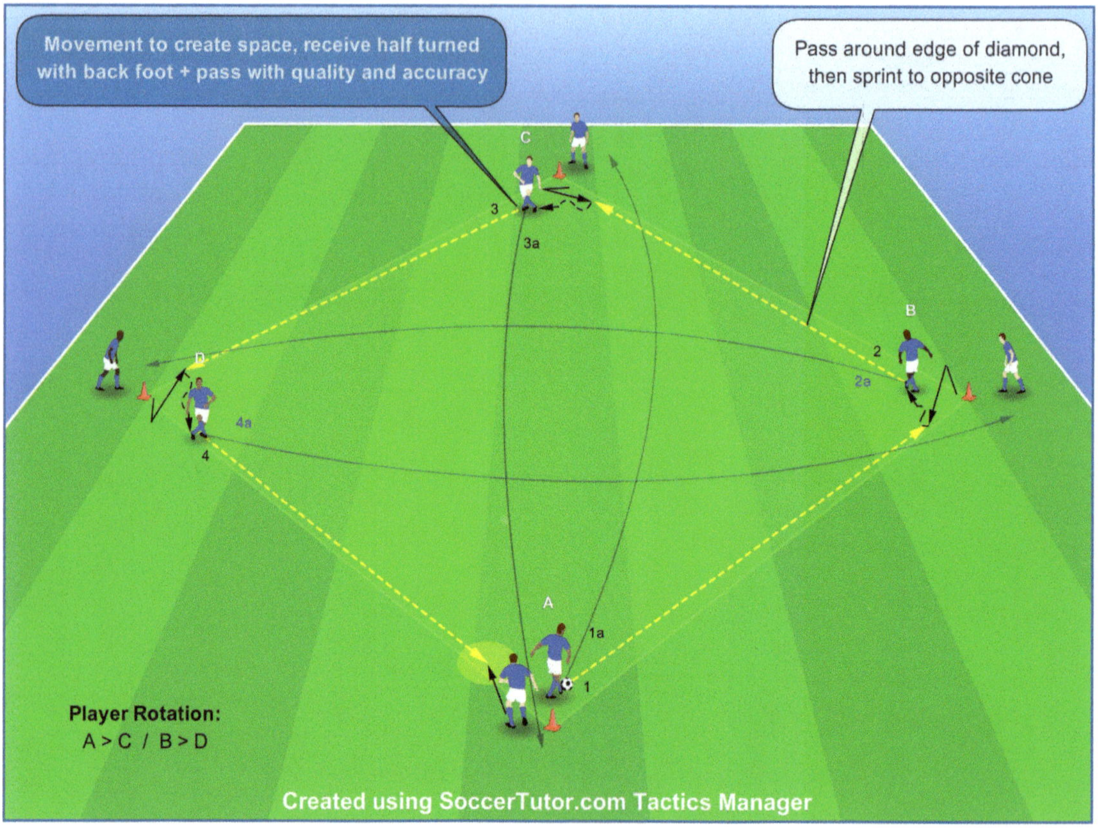

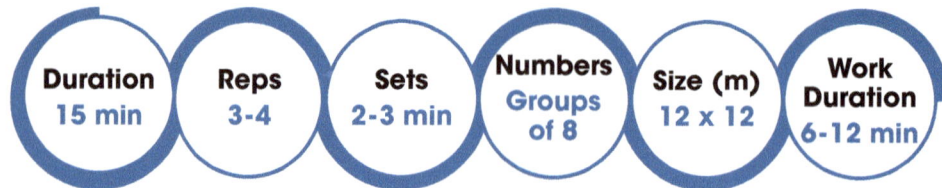

Duration	Reps	Sets	Numbers	Size (m)	Work Duration
15 min	3-4	2-3 min	Groups of 8	12 x 12	6-12 min

OBJECTIVE: Reactions, body shape to receive, and quick accurate passing.

- The players simply pass around the sides of the diamond: **A → B → C → D → A**.
- **Note:** Each player checks away from the cone before moving to receive.
- After their pass, **A** moves to Position C, and **C** moves to Position A. **B** moves to Position D, and **D** moves to Position B.
- The players sprint to the opposite cone (**A → C / B → D**) but must be aware to not collide with other players in the middle.
- **Coaching Point:** Players make double movements to create space, use the correct body shape to receive, and focus on the quality of their passes.

Intensive Technical Practices (Small Spaces)

19. Play Wide and Through Diamond Passing Combinations

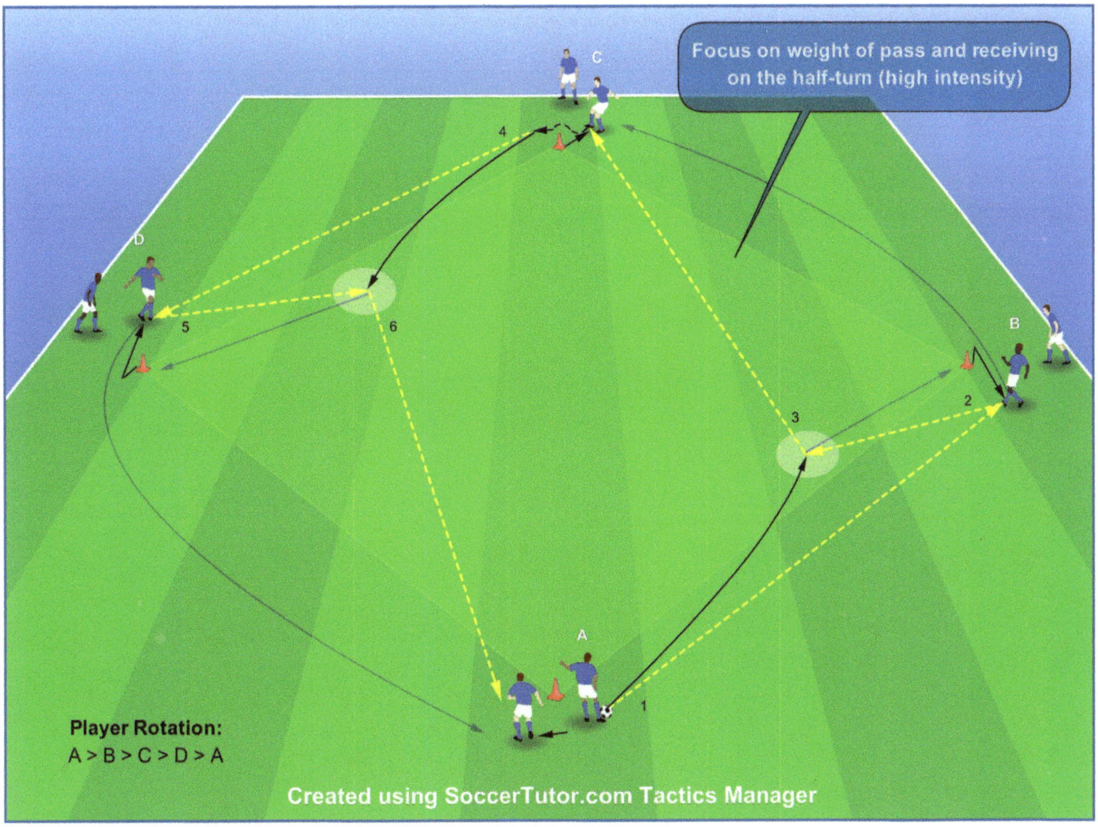

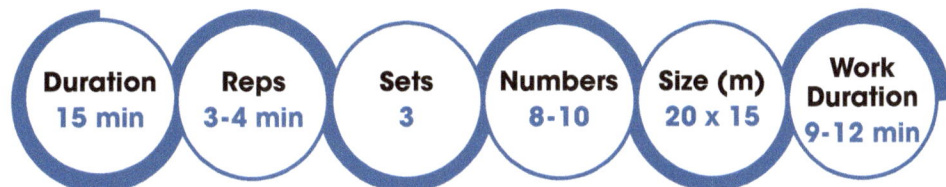

Duration	Reps	Sets	Numbers	Size (m)	Work Duration
15 min	3-4 min	3	8-10	20 x 15	9-12 min

OBJECTIVE: Passing combinations, receiving on the back foot, and body shape.

- **A** passes to **B** and moves to provide support.
- **B** checks away, drops back to receive, and completes a one-two with **A**.
- **A** passes forward (firm ground pass) to **C**, who opens up behind the cone to receive.
- The same sequence repeats with **C** and **D**, ending with **C** passing to the next player waiting at Position A.
- **Coaching Points:** Quality and weight of pass, receive on the half-turn, quick combination play, good movement to receive, and intensity of play/rotations.

Intensive Technical Practices (Small Spaces)

20. High Speed One Touch Diamond Support Play Passing Combinations

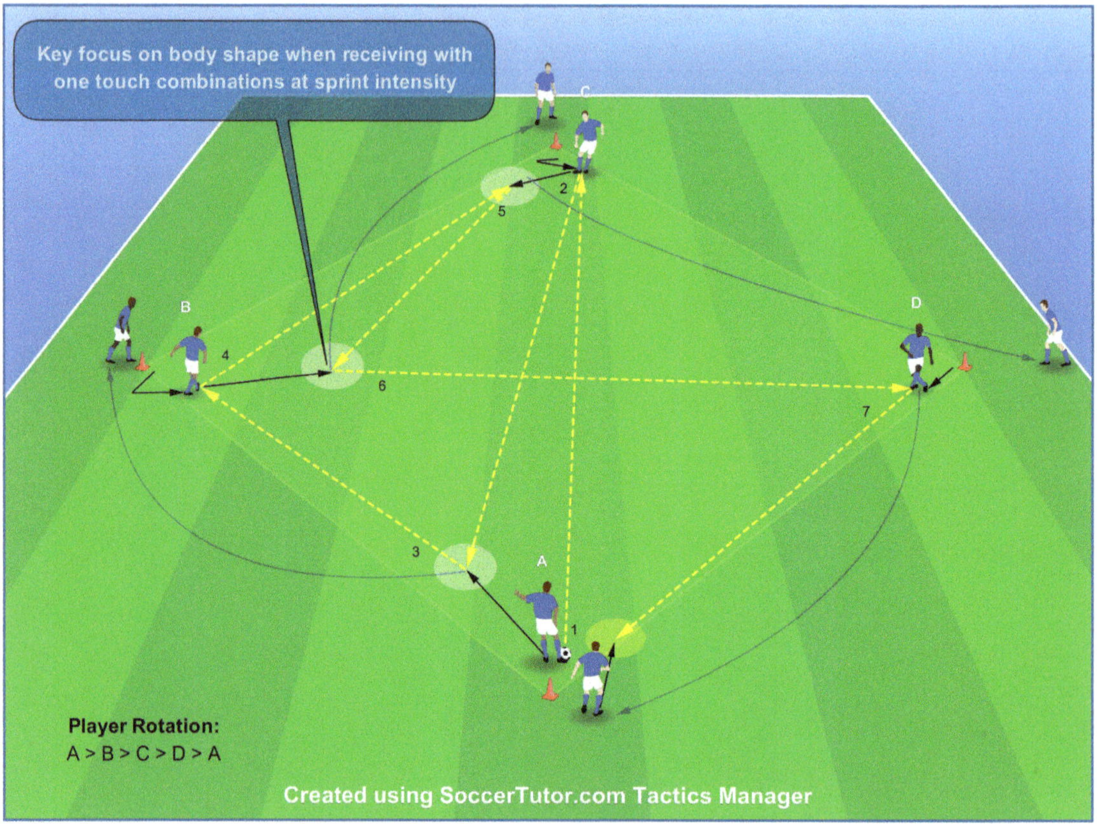

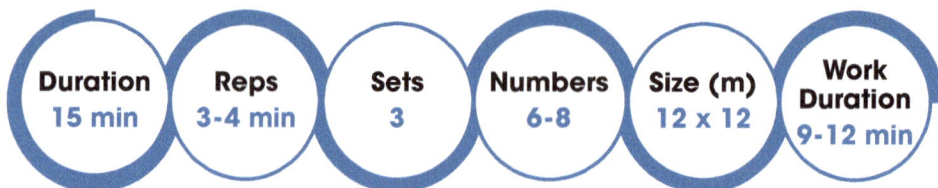

Key focus on body shape when receiving with one touch combinations at sprint intensity

Player Rotation:
A > B > C > D > A

Duration	Reps	Sets	Numbers	Size (m)	Work Duration
15 min	3-4 min	3	6-8	12 x 12	9-12 min

OBJECTIVE: High ball speed, one touch play, and body shape to receive.

- **Simple Starting Sequence:**
  A passes to B, B to C, and C to D, with players following their pass.

- **Progression (Diagram Example):**
  A plays a one-two with C, then passes wide to B, who plays a one-two with C before switching play across to D.

- D passes to Position A (the start) to the next player waiting and the same passing sequence is repeated.

- **Coaching Points:** Focus on quality of pass, high ball speed, player rotation, sprint intensity, and positioning/body shape when receiving.

Intensive Technical Practices (Small Spaces)

21. Inter Milan Passing, Receiving, and Quick Combination Play

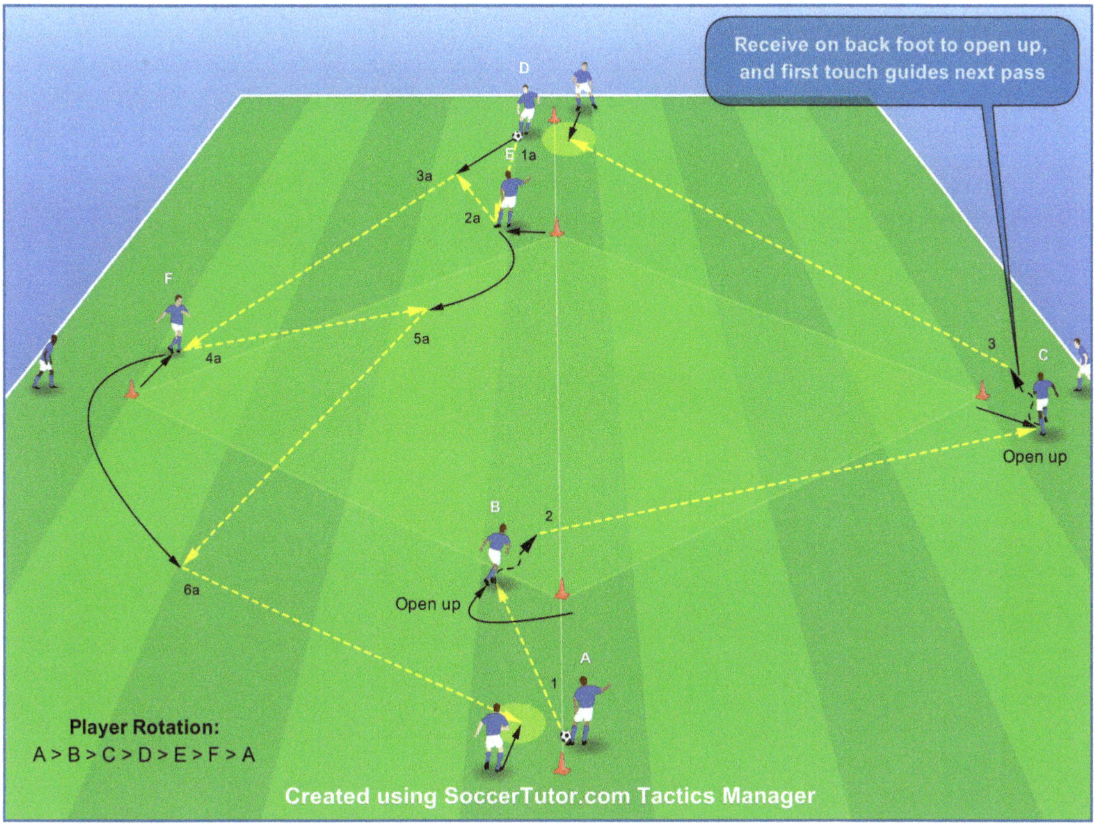

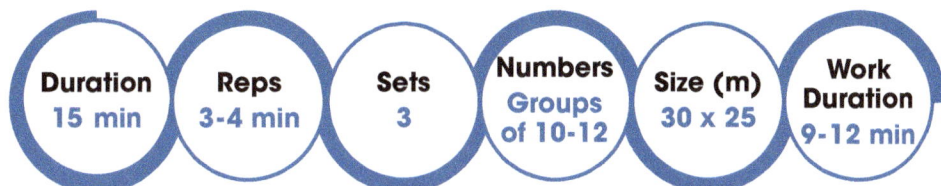

Duration	Reps	Sets	Numbers	Size (m)	Work Duration
15 min	3-4 min	3	Groups of 10-12	30 x 25	9-12 min

OBJECTIVE: Angle of pass, receive on back foot, body shape, and quick combinations.

- Two balls start simultaneously from **A** and **D** and all players follow their pass.
- **A** passes to **B**, who opens up to receive and move forward with the ball, before passing wide to **C**.
- **C** also opens up to receive and passes to the next player waiting at Position D.
- **D** plays a one-two with **E** before passing wide to **F**, who drops off the cone.
- **F** sets the ball for the oncoming **E**, who plays a through pass for **F** to run around the cone and receive (give & go).
- **F** passes to the next player waiting at Position A and the sequence continues.

Intensive Technical Practices (Small Spaces)

22. FC Barcelona Small Spaces "Figure of 8" Progressing Play Combinations

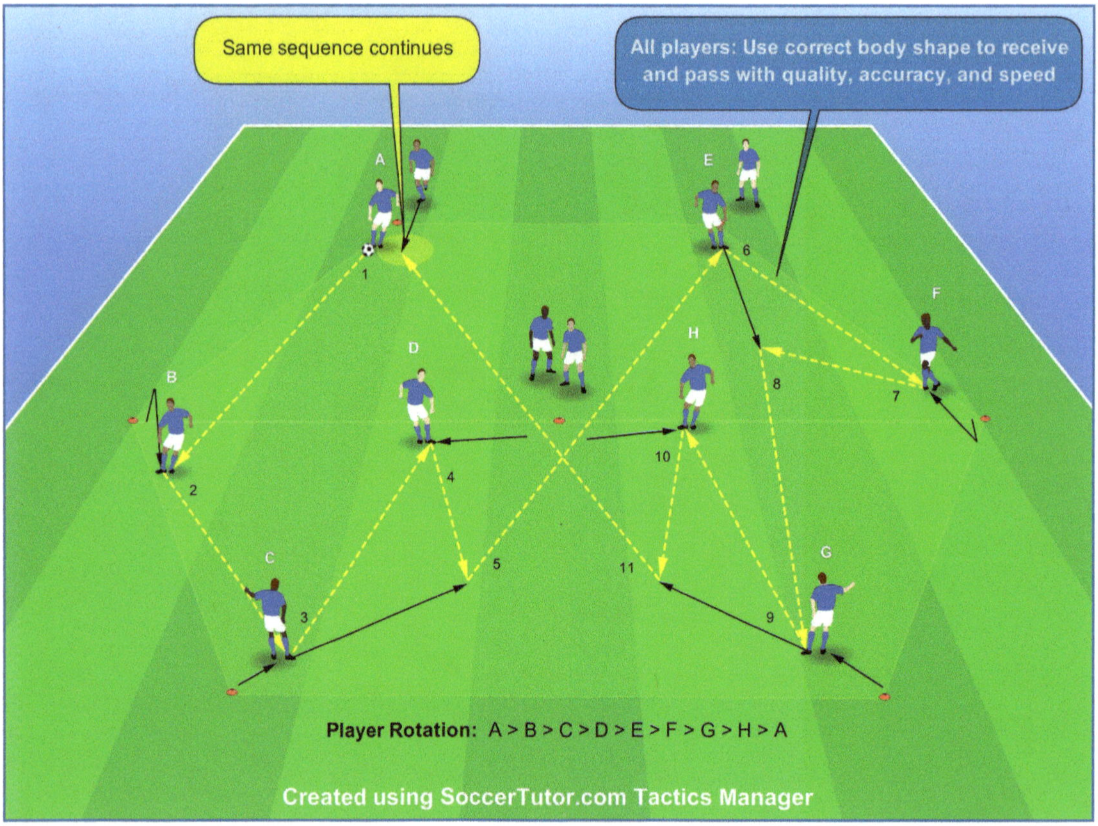

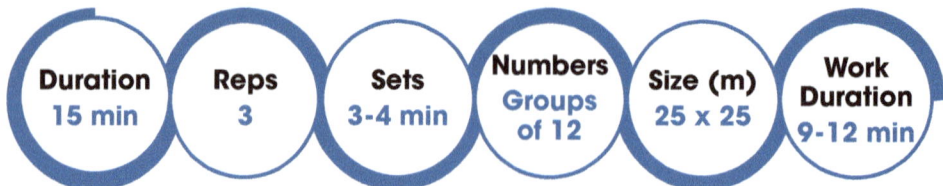

Duration	Reps	Sets	Numbers	Size (m)	Work Duration
15 min	3	3-4 min	Groups of 12	25 x 25	9-12 min

OBJECTIVE: Technical passing/receiving, quick combinations, and through passing.

- **A** passes to **B**, and **B** to **C**. **C** plays a one-two with **D**, and passes diagonally to **E**.
- **E** plays a one-two with **F**, and passes forward to **G**. **G** plays a one-two with **H**, and passes diagonally to Position A.
- All players rotate and the same sequence is started by the next player waiting.
- **Progression:** Add a second ball starting from **E**. **C** and **G** need to be careful to avoid any ball collisions when crossing passes back to the start positions.
- **Coaching Points:** High ball speed, quality passing, and correct body shape to progress the play.

Intensive Technical Practices (Small Spaces)

23. FC Barcelona One-Touch Passing Combinations to Play Forward

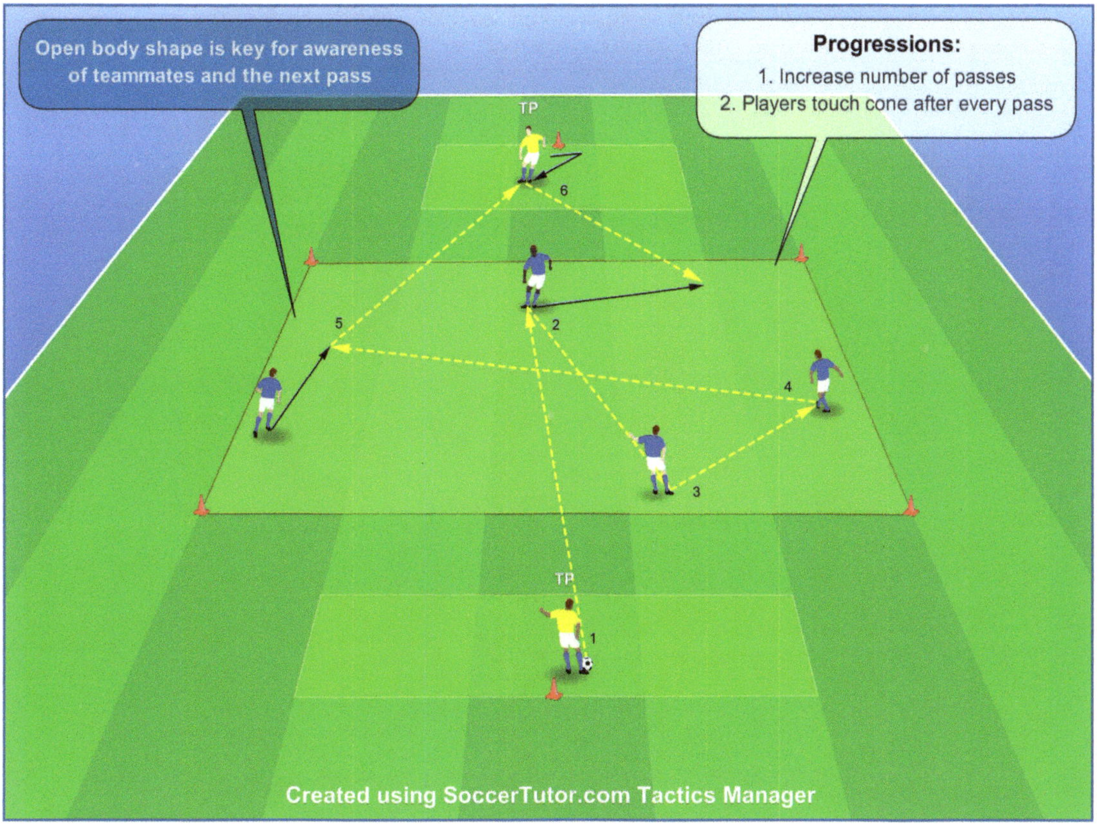

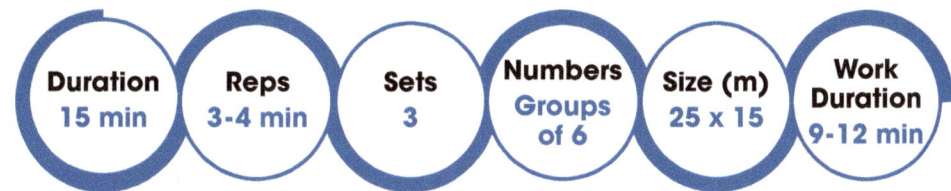

Duration	Reps	Sets	Numbers	Size (m)	Work Duration
15 min	3-4 min	3	Groups of 6	25 x 15	9-12 min

OBJECTIVE: Combinations, one touch passing, and body shape to play forward.

- There are 4 players inside the central box (15 x 15 m) and 1 target player (**TP**) at either end 5 metres from the box.

- A target player (**TP**) starts with a pass into the box. All 4 players must touch the ball (one touch passing) before passing to the target player on the opposite side.

- The practice continues end to end.

- **Progression 1:** Increase the number of passes inside the box.

- **Progression 2:** Add intensity by having players touch a cone after each pass to create space.

Intensive Technical Practices (Small Spaces)

24. Individual Technical Skills: Receiving, Passing, Turning, and Dribbling

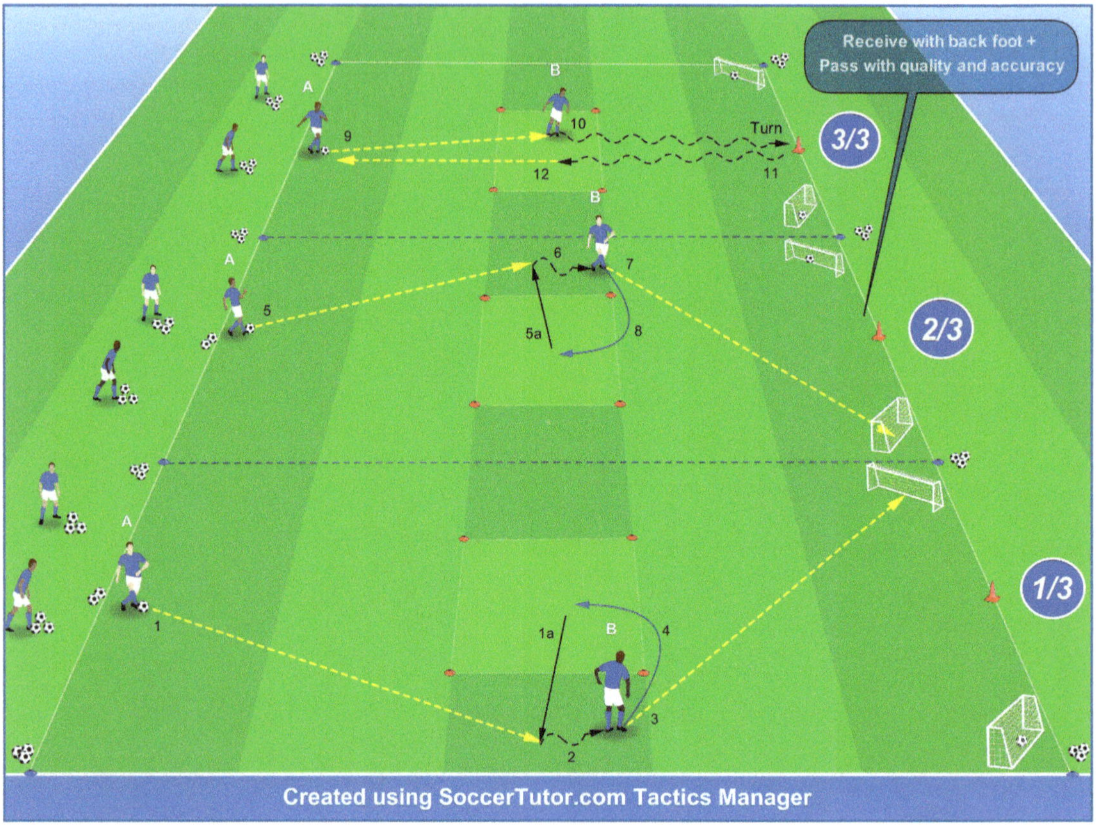

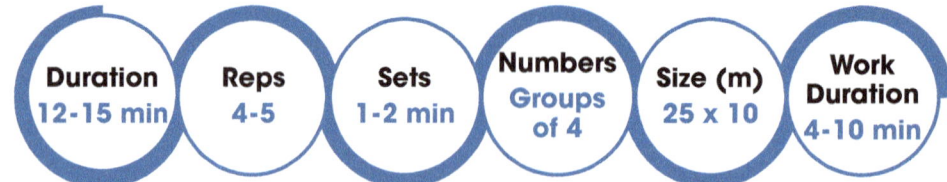

Duration	Reps	Sets	Numbers	Size (m)	Work Duration
12-15 min	4-5	1-2 min	Groups of 4	25 x 10	4-10 min

OBJECTIVE: First touch, reactions, body shape to receive, and quick accurate passing.

- The players work in groups in 25 x 10 m channels with small central squares.
- **A** passes to the right of the square. **B** moves wide to receive, takes a good first touch, and passes into the left goal.
- **B** moves back into the central square and **A** passes to the left of the square.
- **B** moves to receive, takes a good first touch, and passes into the right goal.
- **A** passes into the central square. **B** receives, dribbles to cone, turns, dribbles back into centre, and passes back to **A**.
- **A** moves into central square, **B** moves out, and the next player becomes feeder.

Intensive Technical Practices (Small Spaces)

25. Ladder High Speed Passing, Back Foot Receiving, and Shooting

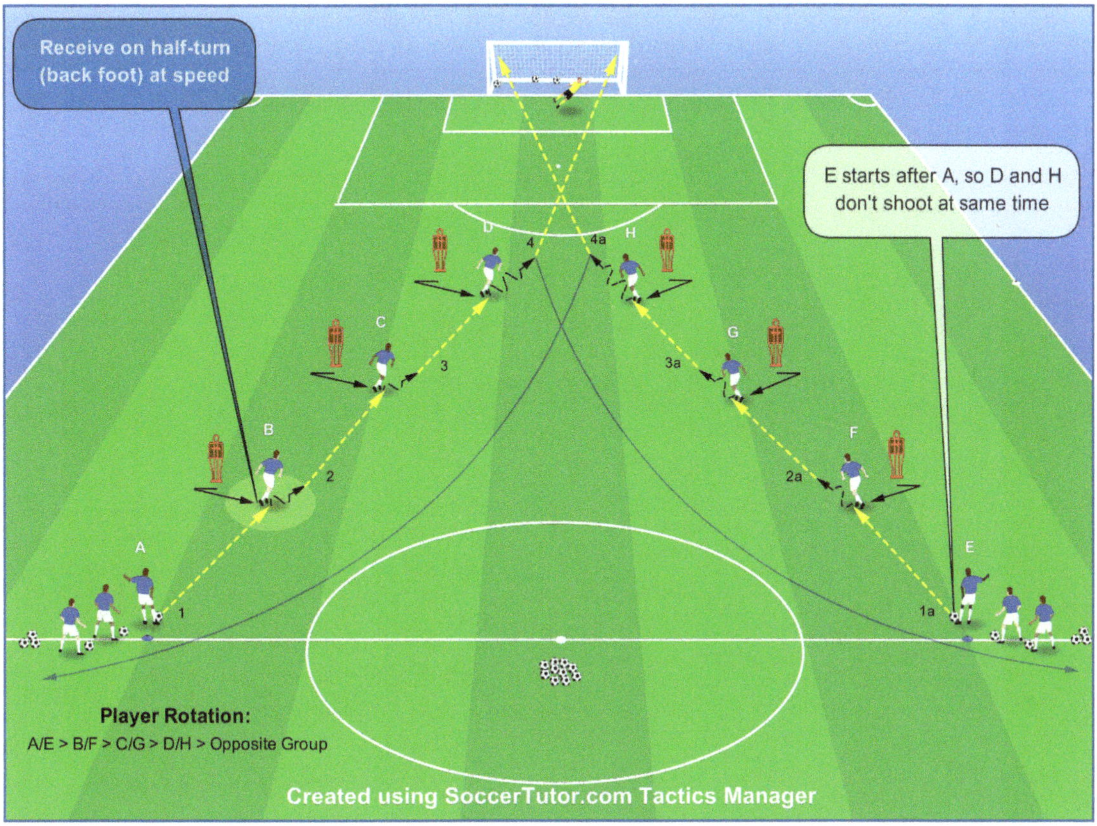

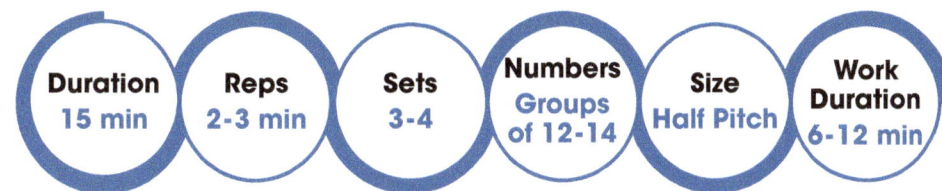

Duration	Reps	Sets	Numbers	Size	Work Duration
15 min	2-3 min	3-4	Groups of 12-14	Half Pitch	6-12 min

OBJECTIVE: High speed passing, body shape, back foot receiving, and shooting.

- This is a simple practice to develop opening up to play forwards.
- Players check off their mannequin to receive with the back foot, turn sharply, pass to the next player, and follow their pass. **D/H** turn and shoot at goal, and then move to the opposite group.

- **Coaching Points:** Quality movement to receive, correct body shape, back foot receiving, and quick decision making.
- **Progression:** Change the sequence to **A/E → C/G → B/F → D/H → C/G → Shoot**. Players **C/G** and **D/H** set the ball back for their oncoming teammates.

Intensive Technical Practices (Small Spaces)

26. Manchester City One-Touch Passing and Finishing Target Goal Race

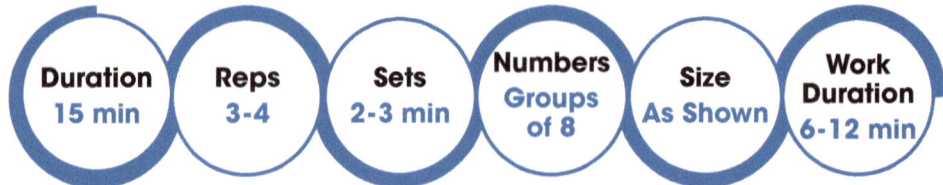

Duration	Reps	Sets	Numbers	Size	Work Duration
15 min	3-4	2-3 min	Groups of 8	As Shown	6-12 min

OBJECTIVE: Body shape, one touch passing, dynamic and accurate finishing.

- The teams of 8 players compete in separate races (A, B, C). The diagram shows all for clarity, though teams race simultaneously.
- **Race 1 (A):** Pass the ball in rotation, moving around the mannequins to receive. When **D** receives, he shoots into a target goal, and the next player goes.
- **Race 2 (B):** Change to **A → C → B → D**, with a switch and **D** opening up behind the mannequin before shooting.
- **Race 3 (C):** One-two, pass, one-two, and through pass by **C** for **D** to shoot.
- The coach can change the direction. The team with the most amount of rotations in a set time wins each race.

Extensive Technical Practices (Large Spaces)

EXTENSIVE TECHNICAL PRACTICES (LARGE SPACES)

Extensive Technical Actions and Practices

In contrast to intensive technical actions, extensive technical actions involve footballing activities that require longer ranges of passing and increased force from a muscle activation standpoint.

These actions are designed to **improve players' ability to execute technical skills over larger areas and longer distances**, emphasising both accuracy and power.

Practices that incorporate extensive technical actions typically require long passing, crossing, and broader movements across larger pitch areas.

Extensive technical actions are typically integrated into the training week on MD +3/-4 (4 days before the match) at the elite professional level - see pages 19-24 for more details for all ages and levels. This is due to the large playing area for these types of practices. These **actions develop technical skills and also enhance players' endurance and muscle strength** due to the increased physical demands.

In this book, we focus on the professional training week. The timing aligns with the microcycle phase methodology, making sure to allow players adequate recovery time before the more intensive training sessions closer to match day.

Extensive technical practices include longer passing combination sequences and/or tactical training e.g. switching play, wide combination play, and large area technical skills e.g. dribbling to break lines.

Players practice passing the ball over longer distances, **focusing on accuracy, power, and proper technique**. They also dribble over extended distances, incorporating changes in pace and direction to simulate match conditions.

NOTE: It is key for players to develop the ability to maintain technical performance over prolonged periods and larger spaces within extensive technical practices.

These Extensive Actions:

- **Enhance players' ability to meet position specific and larger distanced technical demands under pressure**.

- **Replicate the size of match areas and passing patterns, mirroring demands in larger spaces**.

- **Develop decision making by challenging players' technical proficiency in expansive scenarios**.

- **Improve overall technical execution through repeated practice in game relevant contexts**.

Incorporating these practices on specific training days (MD +4/-3) ensures players are physically and mentally primed for peak performance, aligning technical, tactical, and physical readiness.

Extensive Technical Practices (Large Spaces)

Extensive Technical Practices within the Training Week (Microcycle)

Duration	45 min	70-75 min	85-95 min	60-70 min	45-60 min	90 min
Daily Theme	Recovery	Intensive	EXTENSIVE	Intensive	Pre-Match Activation	Match
Preparation	Match Day (MD) +2/-5	Match Day (MD) +3/-4	Match Day (MD) +4/-3	Match Day (MD) +5/-2	Match Day (MD) +6/-1	Match Day
		Positional Principles	Collective Principles	Unit Principles		
Game Type Focus	-	SSGs 1v1-4v4 (+GKs) Small Area	LSGs 8v8-10v10 (+GKs) Large Area	MSGs 5v5-7v7 (+GKs) Medium Area	LSGs 8v8-10v10 (+GKs) Small/Med Area	Match Day 11v11
Bout Durations	-	1-3 min	5-10 min	3-5 min	4 min	2 x 45 min
	Mon: Recovery	Tue-Wed: Conditioning		Thu-Fri: Preparation		Perform

* Training Week based on Professional Microcycle Example - *see pages 19-20.*

- **Extensive Technical Practices** are used on **MD +4/-3** within the training week, which is 4 days after the previous match day and 3 days before the next one.

- **3 Days Until Match (MD +4/-3):**
  Collective Team Principle Training with Extensive Technical Practices

  * See next page full training session outline.

Extensive Technical Practices (Large Spaces)

Extensive Technical Training Session
3 Days Until Match (MD +4/-3) Example

Collective Team Principle and Extensive Technical Training Session (85-95 min):

1. Speed Endurance Warm Up (10-12 min)
2. Extensive Technical Practice (12-15 min)
3. Speed Endurance Conditioning Practice (5-15 min)
4. Large Sided Possession (10-15 min)
5. Large Sided Game in Large Area (10-50 min)

* **Based on Professional Training Week (Microcycle)** - see pages 19-24 for other ages/levels.

Extensive Technical Practices (Large Spaces)

MD +4/-3
Extensive Technical Practices

Longer Passing
Players practice passing the ball over longer distances, focusing on accuracy, power, and proper technique e.g. Switching play from one side of the pitch to the other.

Larger Area Technical Skills
Receiving, dribbling over larger distances, and finishing in match-like situations.

Tactical Training
With larger playing areas, tactical topics such as build up play, breaking lines, wide combination play, etc are included.

Why are Extensive Technical Practices Used on the MD +4/-3 Day of the Training Week?
They are often used earlier in the training week (microcycle), allowing players adequate recovery time before the more intensive sessions closer to match day.

How Does this Help to Maximise Performance?
These extensive technical practices are crucial for developing the ability to maintain technical performance over prolonged periods and larger spaces.

Extensive Technical Practices (Large Spaces)

Key Coaching Points for Extensive Technical Practices (Large Spaces)

Larger Surface Areas and Greater Distances
- Use larger spaces on MD +4/-3 to cover more ground.
- Simulate match related conditions.
- Reinforce tactical awareness and spatial positioning.

Tactical Relevance and Position Specific Details
- Focus on game-like passes tailored to specific match situations.
- Align practices with player specific positional roles.
- Ensure tactical and technical match preparation.

Repetition of Forceful Actions
- Incorporate longer, powerful passes to build strength.
- Develop precision for high intensity match situations.
- Enhance technical consistency through repetition.

Increased Physical Demands
- Use greater distances and higher ball speeds to boost workload.
- Promote speed endurance and match intensity.
- Align practices with MD +4/-3 physiological goals.

Extensive Technical Practices (Large Spaces)

1. Receiving Under Pressure and Dribbling Skills Passing "Y"

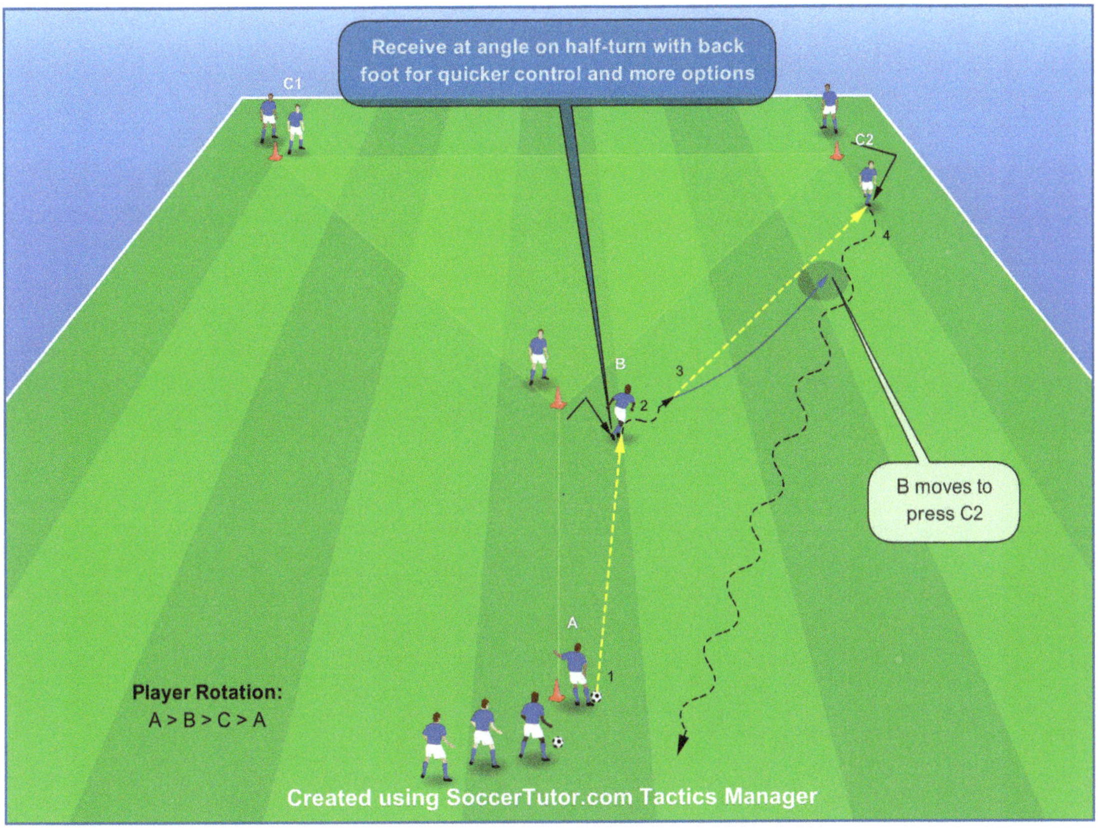

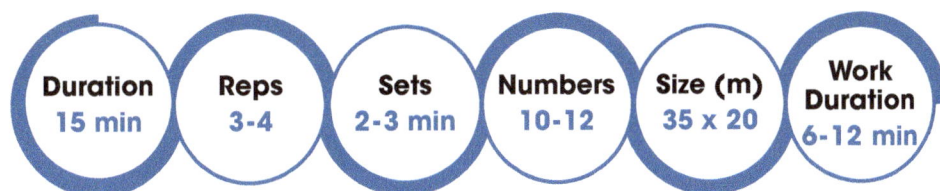

Duration	Reps	Sets	Numbers	Size (m)	Work Duration
15 min	3-4	2-3 min	10-12	35 x 20	6-12 min

OBJECTIVE: Forward passing, receiving on the half-turn, pressing, and dribbling.

- **A** passes to **B**, who checks off the cone before moving to receive.

- **B** receives on the half-turn, and then passes to **C2**.

- **B** sprints to (passively) press **C2**, who dribbles to the start Position A to complete the sequence.

- The next player waiting enters with a new ball and the same sequence is repeated. This time, **B** will receive a pass on the left side and pass to **C1**.

- **Progression:** **C** plays a one-two with **B**, and then plays a lofted pass to the next player waiting at Position A.

©SOCCERTUTOR.COM   Technical to Maximise Performance

Extensive Technical Practices (Large Spaces)

2. Changing Lines and Angles Passing Combinations and Support Play

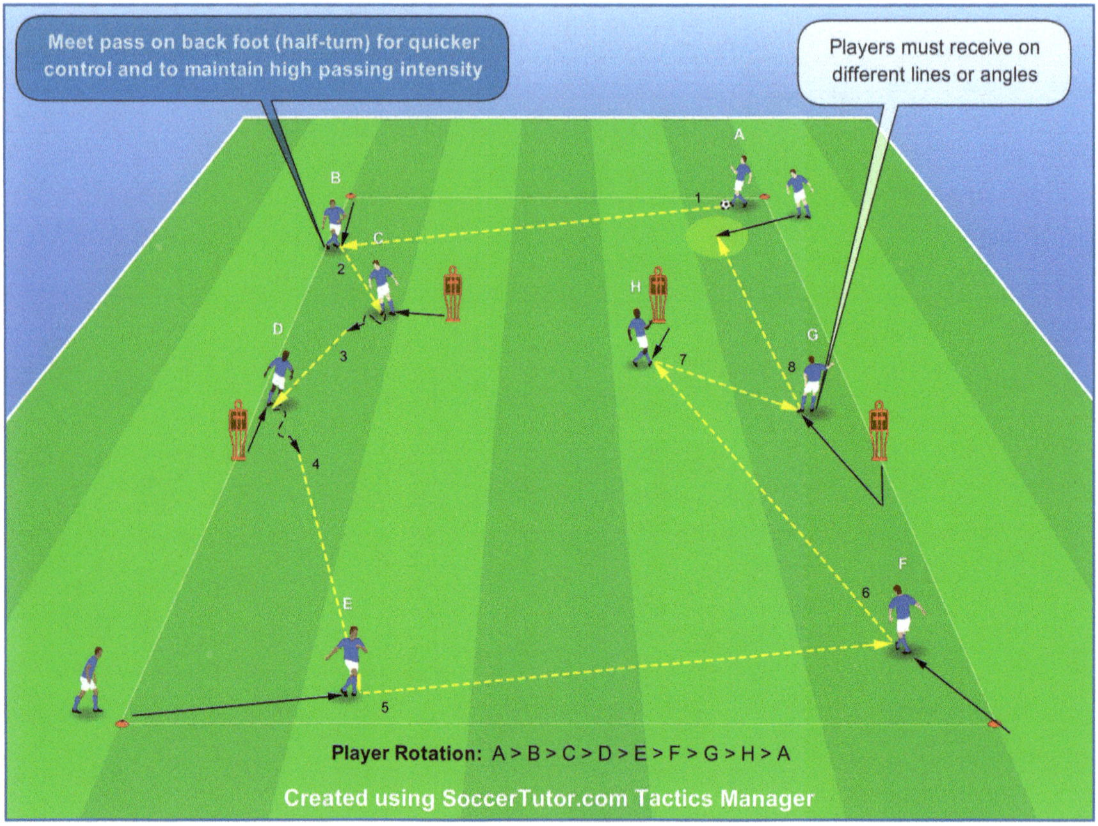

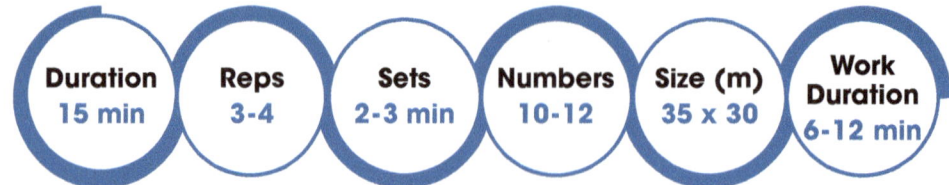

Duration	Reps	Sets	Numbers	Size (m)	Work Duration
15 min	3-4	2-3 min	10-12	35 x 30	6-12 min

OBJECTIVE: Forward passing, combination play, and receiving on the back foot.

- **Note:** The players must be on different lines and/or angles to receive.
- **A** passes to **B**, and **B** passes to **C**, who moves off the mannequin, receives, turns, and passes to **D**. **D** does the same and passes to **E**, who moves inside off the cone, and passes to **F**.
- **F** passes forward to **H**, who sets the ball for **G** (double movement) to pass to the next player waiting at Position A, and the same sequence is repeated.
- **Coaching Points:** Weight of pass, correct execution of half-turn, smooth rotations, and high intensity throughout.

Extensive Technical Practices (Large Spaces)

3. PSG Switching Play Passing and Receiving Rotations

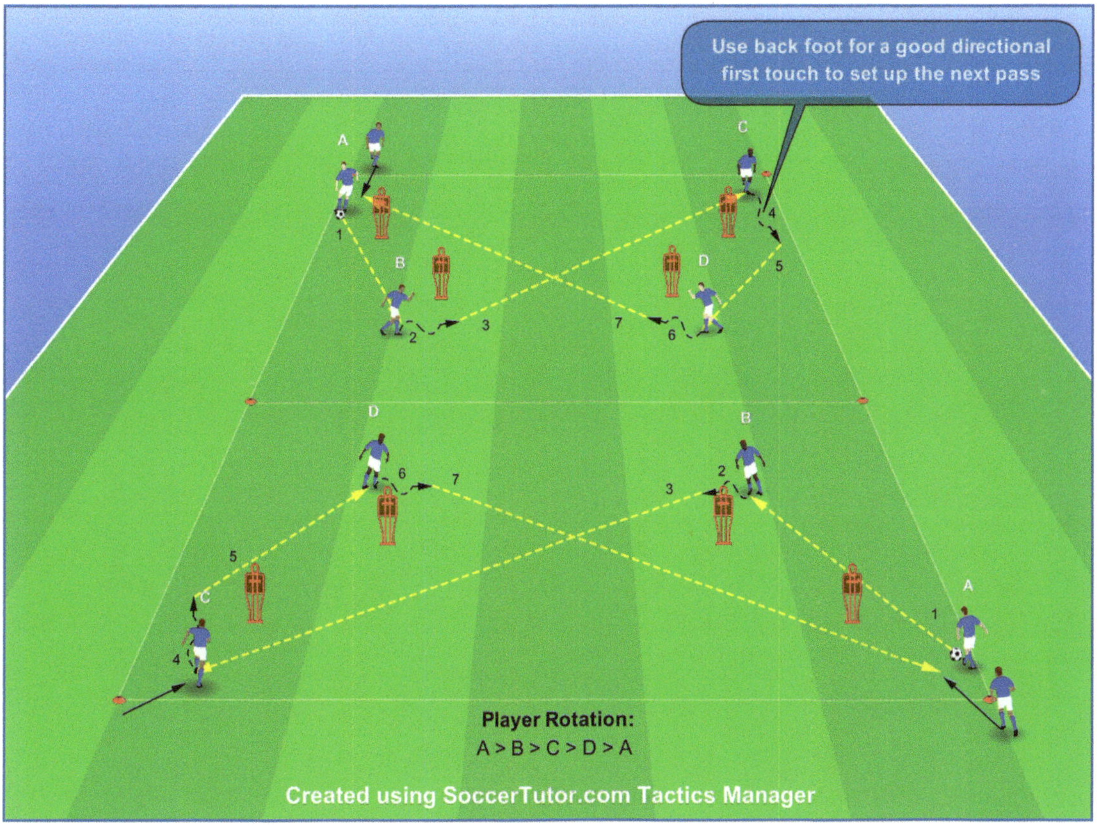

[Diagram: Use back foot for a good directional first touch to set up the next pass. Player Rotation: A > B > C > D > A. Created using SoccerTutor.com Tactics Manager]

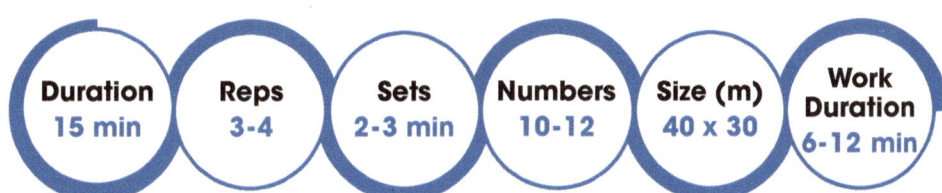

Duration	Reps	Sets	Numbers	Size (m)	Work Duration
15 min	3-4	2-3 min	10-12	40 x 30	6-12 min

OBJECTIVE: Technical passing patterns with a focus on switching play.

- In each half of the area, there are 5-6 players and 4 positioned mannequins.
- **A** passes to **B**, who opens up to receive and switch the play (diagonal pass) to **C**.
- **C** also opens up and receives around the mannequin. **C** passes to **D**, who does the same.
- **D** completes the sequence with a diagonal switch pass to the next player waiting at Position A.
- The same sequence repeats.
- **Coaching Points:** Effective passing and receiving techniques, with a focus on control and accuracy throughout.

Extensive Technical Practices (Large Spaces)

4. Technical Rotational Passing Race (Progressive Pattern)

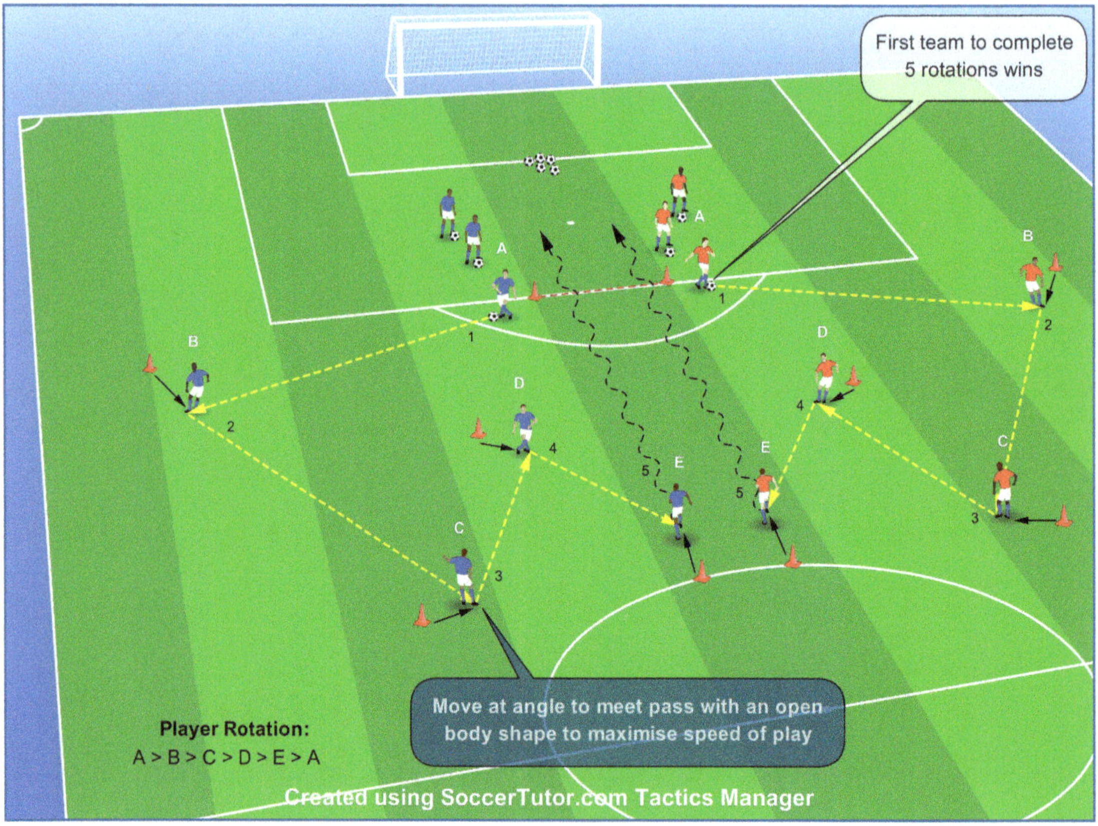

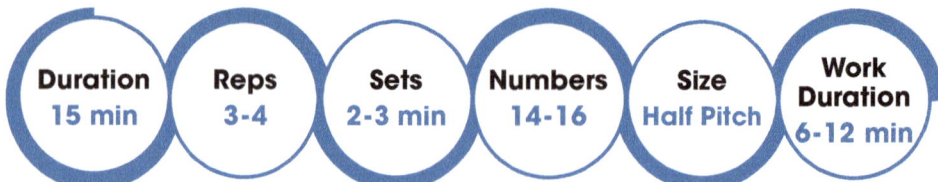

First team to complete 5 rotations wins

Move at angle to meet pass with an open body shape to maximise speed of play

Player Rotation:
A > B > C > D > E > A

Duration	Reps	Sets	Numbers	Size	Work Duration
15 min	3-4	2-3 min	14-16	Half Pitch	6-12 min

OBJECTIVE: Forward passing, tactical combinations, and progressive passing patterns.

- The players are split into two teams. In this example, each team has 7 players.
- The players pass through the rotation: **A → B → C → D → E**.
- When **E** receives, they must dribble through the cone gate before the next player (new ball at Position A) can start.
- The teams are in competition to see who can complete 5 ball rotations first.
- The 5 rotations must be completed consecutively without any mistakes.
- **Progressions:** Increase difficulty by changing the combinations and/or movements, or limit to e.g. left foot only.

Extensive Technical Practices (Large Spaces)

5. FC Barcelona "Figure of 8" Progressing Play Combinations and Support Play

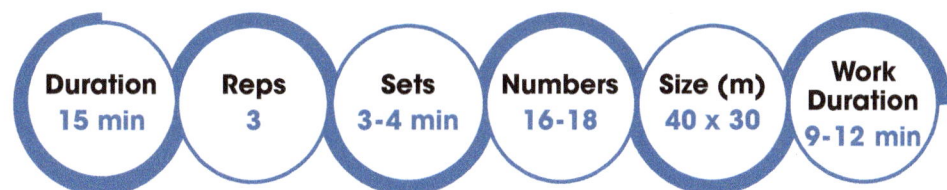

Player Rotation:
A > B > C > D > E > F > G > H > A

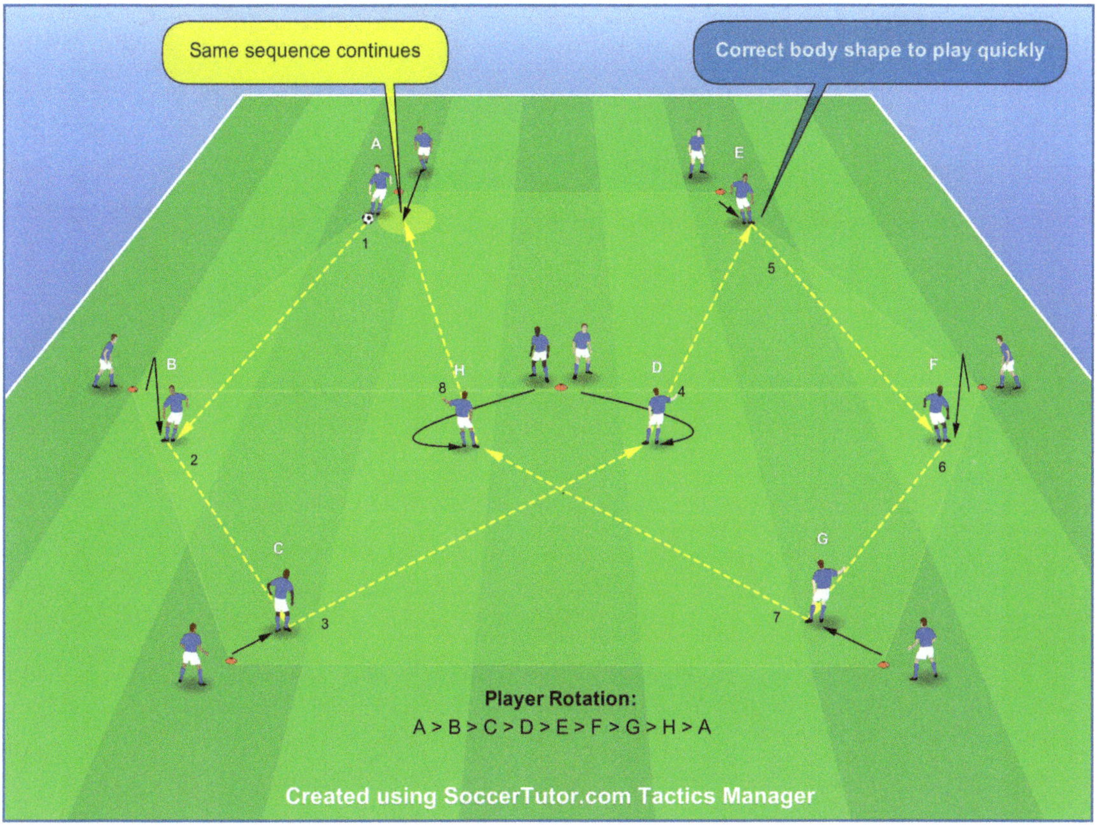

Duration	Reps	Sets	Numbers	Size (m)	Work Duration
15 min	3	3-4 min	16-18	40 x 30	9-12 min

OBJECTIVE: Technical passing/receiving, quick combinations, and support play.

- **A** passes to **B**, and **B** to **C**.
- **C** passes inside (diagonally) to **D**, who drops back and opens up to receive and progress the play with a pass to **E**.
- The same sequence is then repeated as a mirror image on the opposite side: E → F → G → H → Position A.

- **Progression:** Add a second ball starting from **E**. **D** and **H** need to be careful to avoid any collisions with each other or the balls when crossing passes.
- **Coaching Points:** High ball speed, quality passing, and correct body shape to play out.

Extensive Technical Practices (Large Spaces)

6. FC Barcelona "Figure of 8" Progressing Play Combinations and Support Play (Progression)

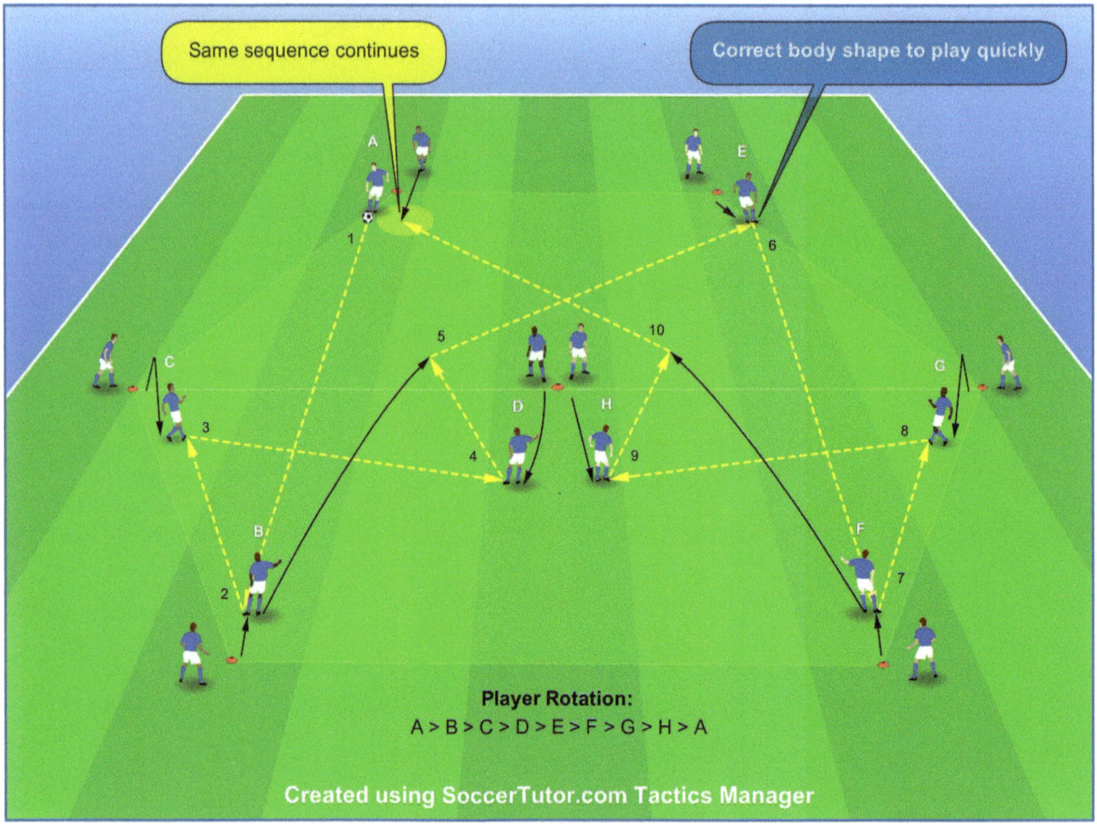

[Diagram of practice setup with players A–H arranged across a 40x30 area. Annotations: "Same sequence continues" and "Correct body shape to play quickly". Player Rotation: A > B > C > D > E > F > G > H > A]

Duration	Reps	Sets	Numbers	Size (m)	Work Duration
15 min	3	3-4 min	14-16	40 x 30	9-12 min

OBJECTIVE: Technical passing/receiving, quick combination play, and support runs.

- **A** passes to **B**, who sets the ball back for **C** after a double movement. **C** passes inside to **D**, who drops back to receive. **D** passes for the third man supporting run of **B**, who passes across to **E**.

- The same sequence is then repeated as a mirror image on the opposite side: E → F → G → H → F → Position A.

- The same sequence starts with the next player waiting as all players have followed their pass to the next position.

- **Coaching Points:** Effective passing and receiving, with a focus on control and accuracy, timing of movements to receive, and correct body shape to play.

Extensive Technical Practices (Large Spaces)

7. Ajax One-Twos, Movement, Timing, and Positional Passing

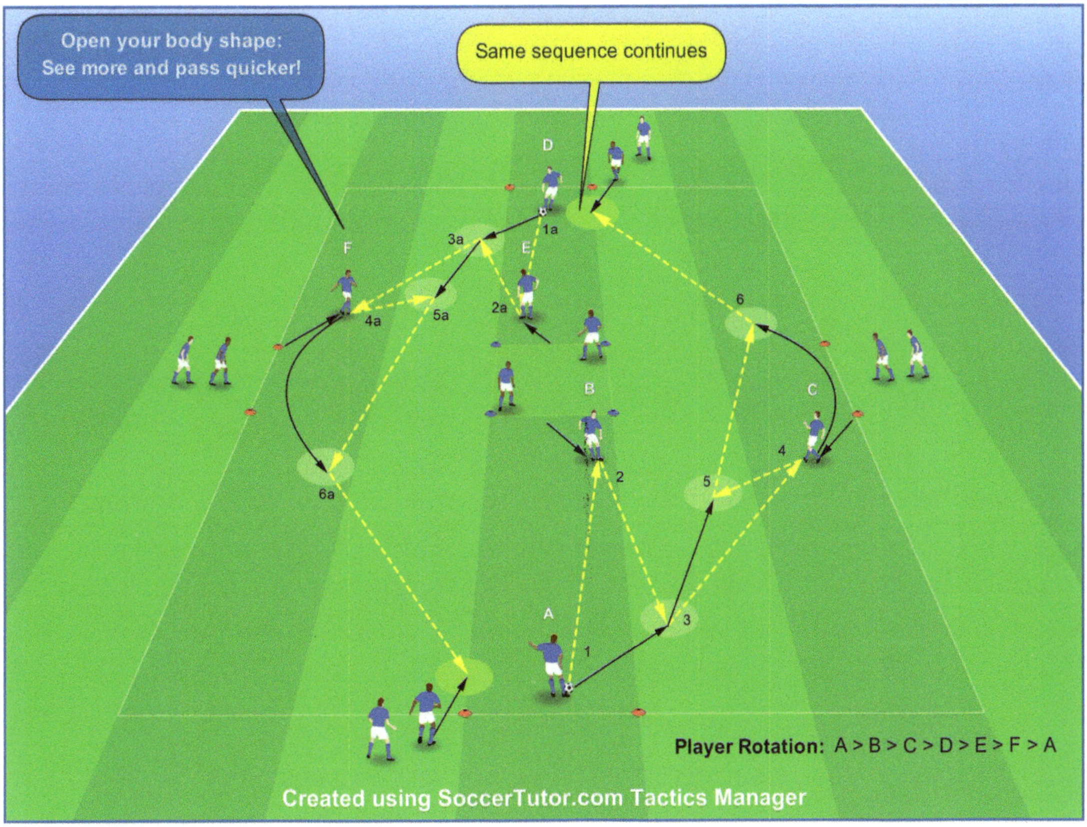

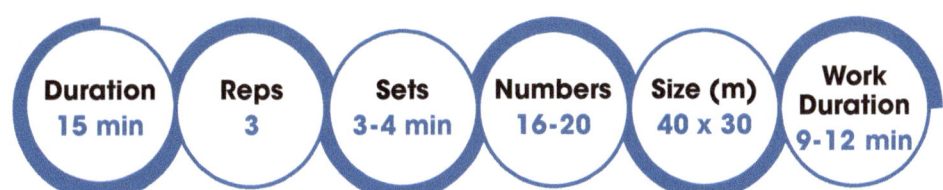

Duration	Reps	Sets	Numbers	Size (m)	Work Duration
15 min	3	3-4 min	16-20	40 x 30	9-12 min

OBJECTIVE: Movement, timing, body shape to receive, and positional passing.

- In the 40 x 30 m area, mark out cone gates in a diamond shape and a small central square. The circuit starts with 2 balls simultaneously from **A** and **D**.
- **A/D** play a one-two with **B/E**, who set the ball back for **A/D** to pass to **C/F**.
- **C/F** play a give & go with **A/D**.
- **C/F** completes the sequence by passing to Position A/D for the next player waiting. The same sequence repeats.
- **Variation:** When **C/F** set the ball back to **A/D**, they instead play a long pass to the next players waiting at Position A/D to complete the sequence.

Extensive Technical Practices (Large Spaces)

8. Rotational Passing Combinations with Overlap Third Man Runs

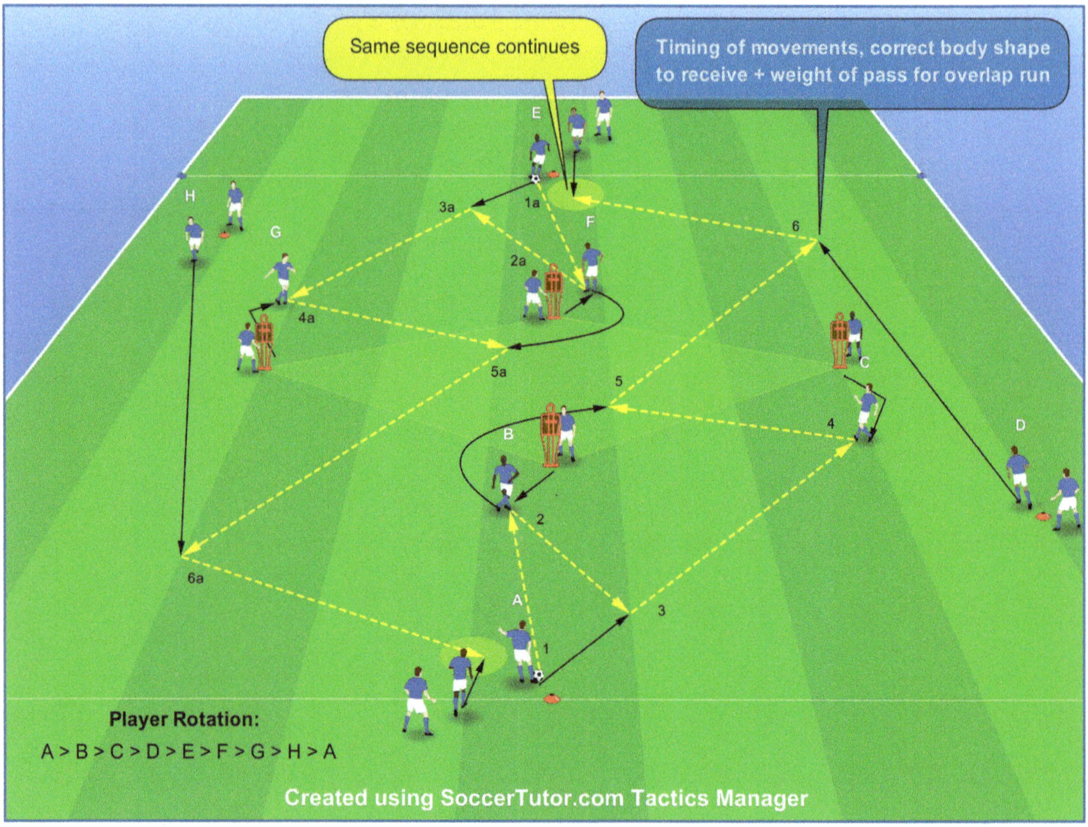

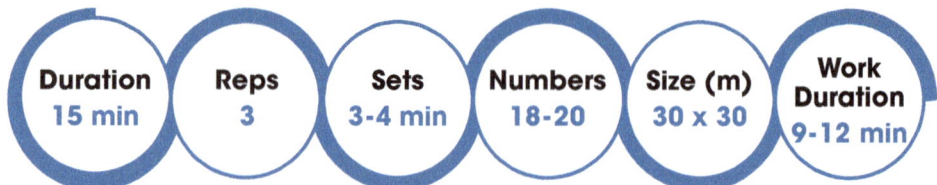

Duration	Reps	Sets	Numbers	Size (m)	Work Duration
15 min	3	3-4 min	18-20	30 x 30	9-12 min

OBJECTIVE: Technical passing/receiving, quick combination play, and third man runs.

- Two balls start simultaneously from **A** and **E**. **A/E** play a one-two with **B/F**, then pass wide to **C/G**.

- **C/G** pass inside to **B/F**, who run around the mannequin to provide support.

- **B/F** then play a through pass for the overlapping third man run of **D/H**.

- **D/H** finish with a pass to Position A/E.

- **Coaching Points:** Effective passing and receiving, with a focus on control and accuracy. Timing of movements to receive and correct body shape to play is key, as well as the weight of pass (**B/F**) for the overlapping player (**D/H**).

Extensive Technical Practices (Large Spaces)

9. High Intensity Game Speed Build Up Play Technical Circuit

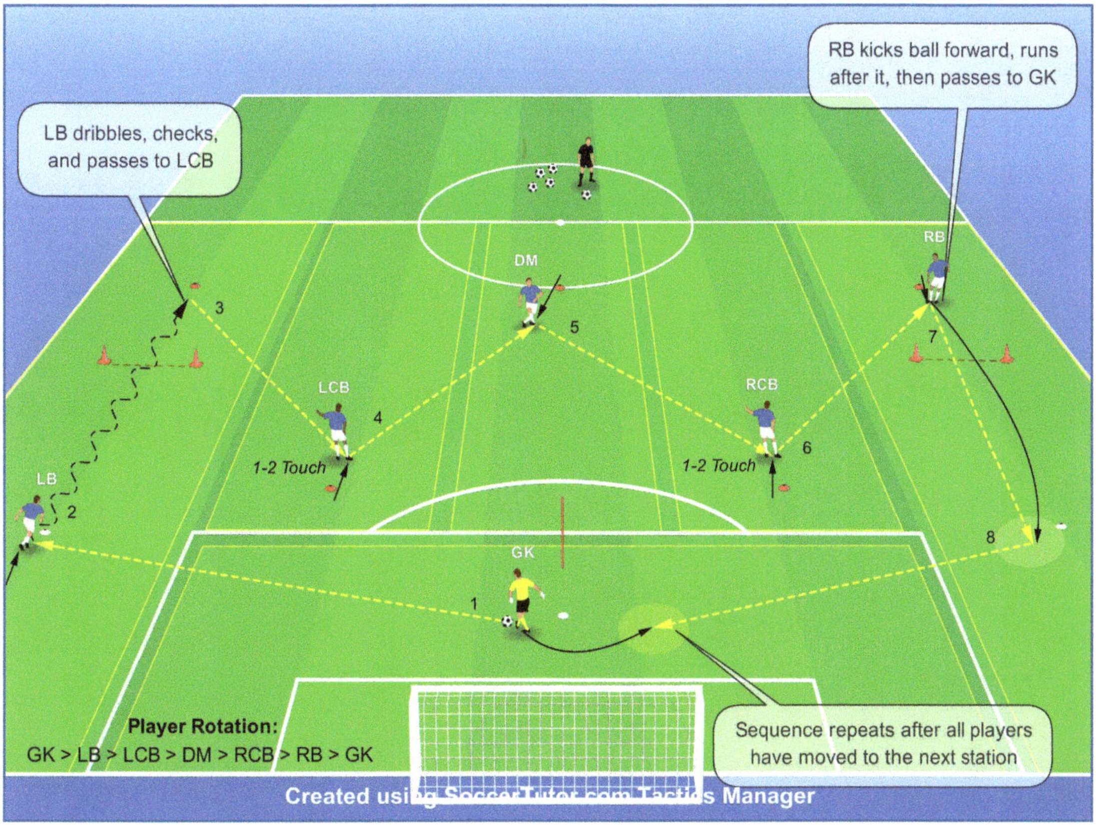

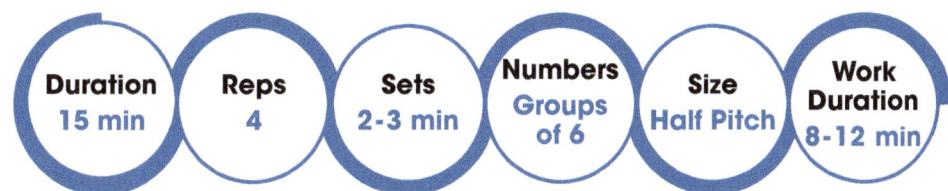

Duration	Reps	Sets	Numbers	Size	Work Duration
15 min	4	2-3 min	Groups of 6	Half Pitch	8-12 min

OBJECTIVE: Build up play skills - passing, receiving, dribbling, and movements.

- The ball is played from station to station. **GK** passes wide to start. **LB** receives and dribbles forward, stops/checks, then passes to **LCB**. **LCB**, **DM**, and **RCB** receive and pass to the next player. **RB** receives, kicks the ball forward and runs to it, before completing the sequence with a final pass back to **GK**.

- All players move into the next station, following the circuit as it continues: **GK → LB → LCB → DM → RCB → RB → GK**.

- **Coaching Points:** Effective passing and receiving techniques. Focus on control and accuracy throughout, while attempting a high speed of play.

Extensive Technical Practices (Large Spaces)

10. High Intensity Game Speed Build Up Play Technical Circuit (Free Decision Making)

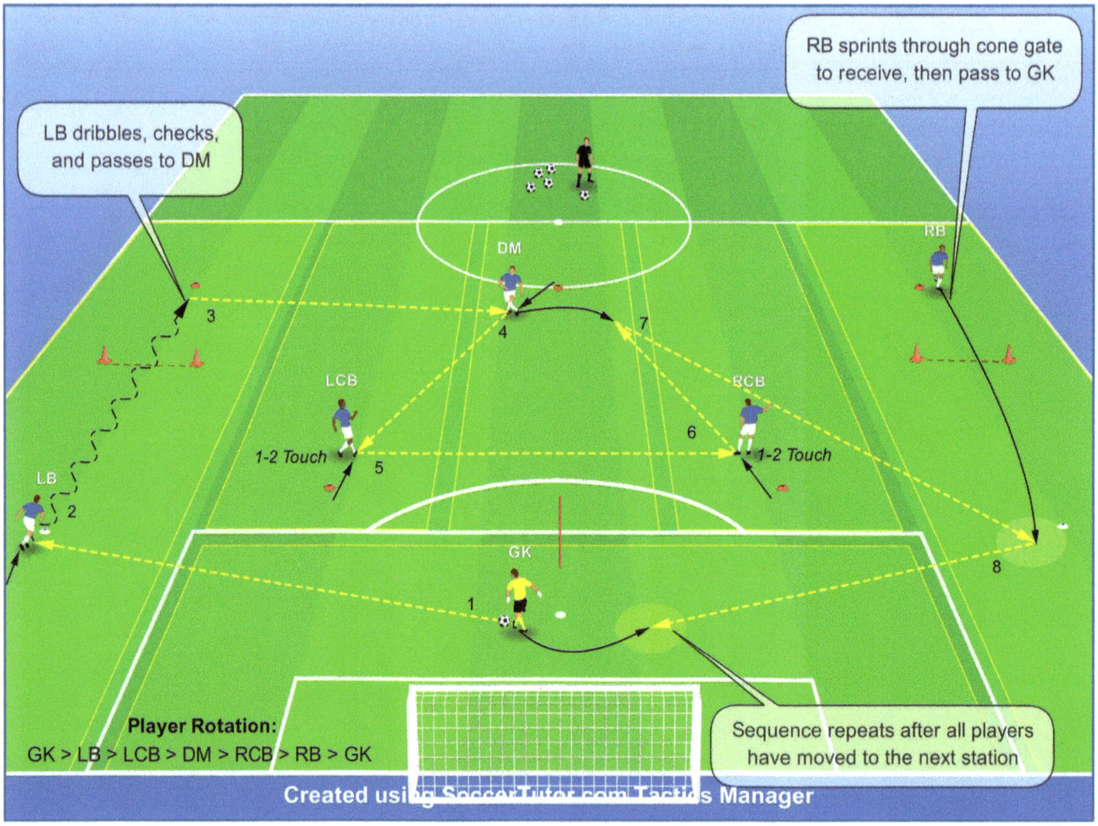

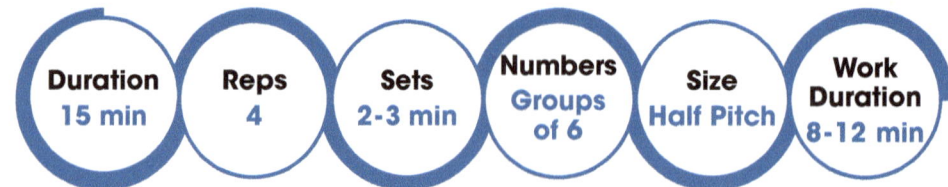

Duration	Reps	Sets	Numbers	Size	Work Duration
15 min	4	2-3 min	Groups of 6	Half Pitch	8-12 min

OBJECTIVE: Build up play skills - passing, receiving, dribbling, and movements.

- In this variation of the previous practice, we remove the limitations of a set sequence.
- The players can now vary the types of combinations as they have free decision making.
- The diagram shows one example of this.
- All players still move to the next station, following the circuit as it continues: GK → LB → LCB → DM → RCB → RB → GK.
- **Coaching Points:** Emphasise quick decision making under pressure, accurate passing and receiving, and effective communication.

Extensive Technical Practices (Large Spaces)

11. Play Out from the Back Tactical Rotational Passing Combinations

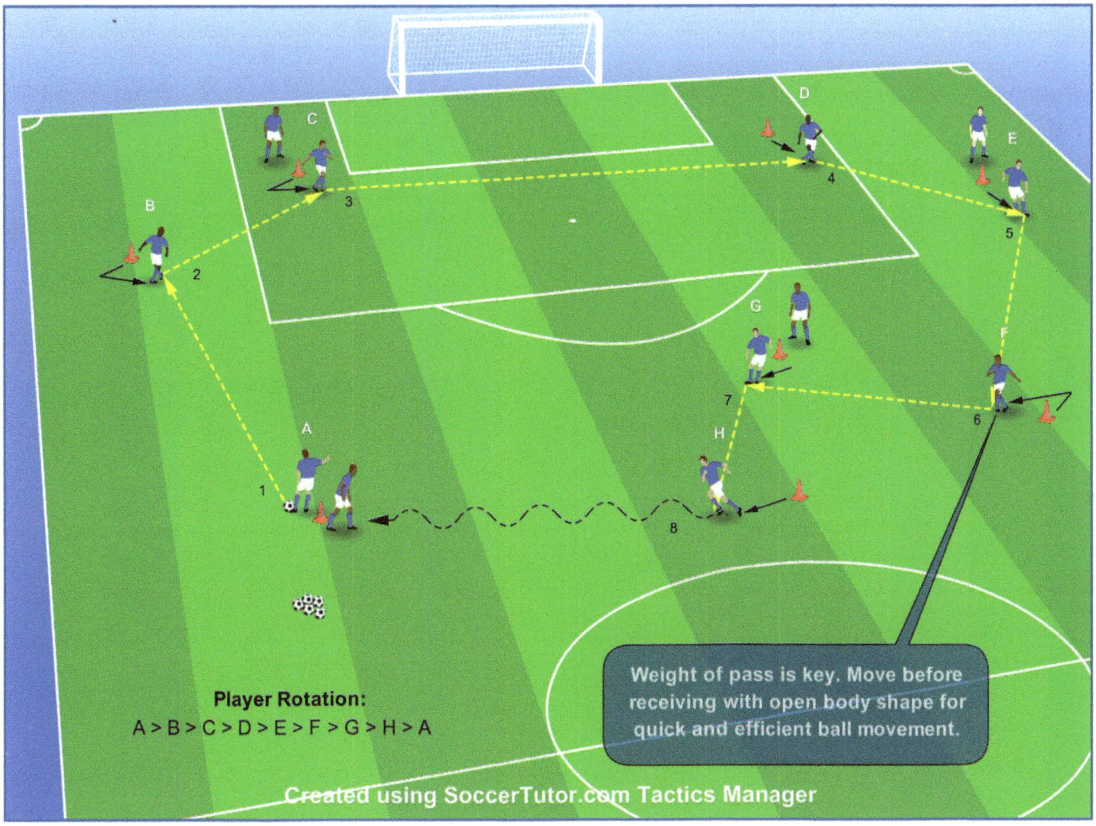

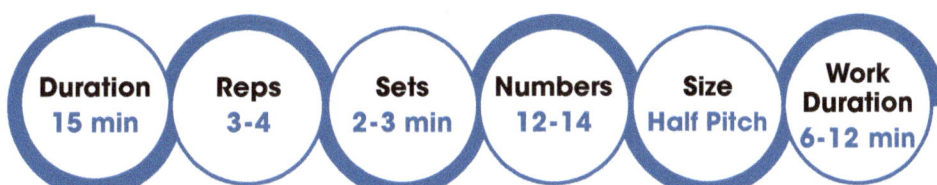

Player Rotation:
A > B > C > D > E > F > G > H > A

Weight of pass is key. Move before receiving with open body shape for quick and efficient ball movement.

Created using SoccerTutor.com Tactics Manager

Duration	Reps	Sets	Numbers	Size	Work Duration
15 min	3-4	2-3 min	12-14	Half Pitch	6-12 min

OBJECTIVE: Forward passing, tactical combinations, and progressive running with ball.

- The players pass through the rotation:
  A → B → C → D → E → F → G → H → A.
- When **H** receives, he must dribble the ball as quickly as possible to deliver the ball to the player waiting at Position A. That player then turns and starts the next rotation.

Progressions:

1. Increase the difficulty by changing the combinations and/or movements, or limit to e.g. left or right foot only.
2. If you have the numbers, have two teams compete to see who can complete 5-7 rotations first.

©SOCCERTUTOR.COM   Technical to Maximise Performance

Extensive Technical Practices (Large Spaces)

12. Two Team Positional Build Up Passing Sequences

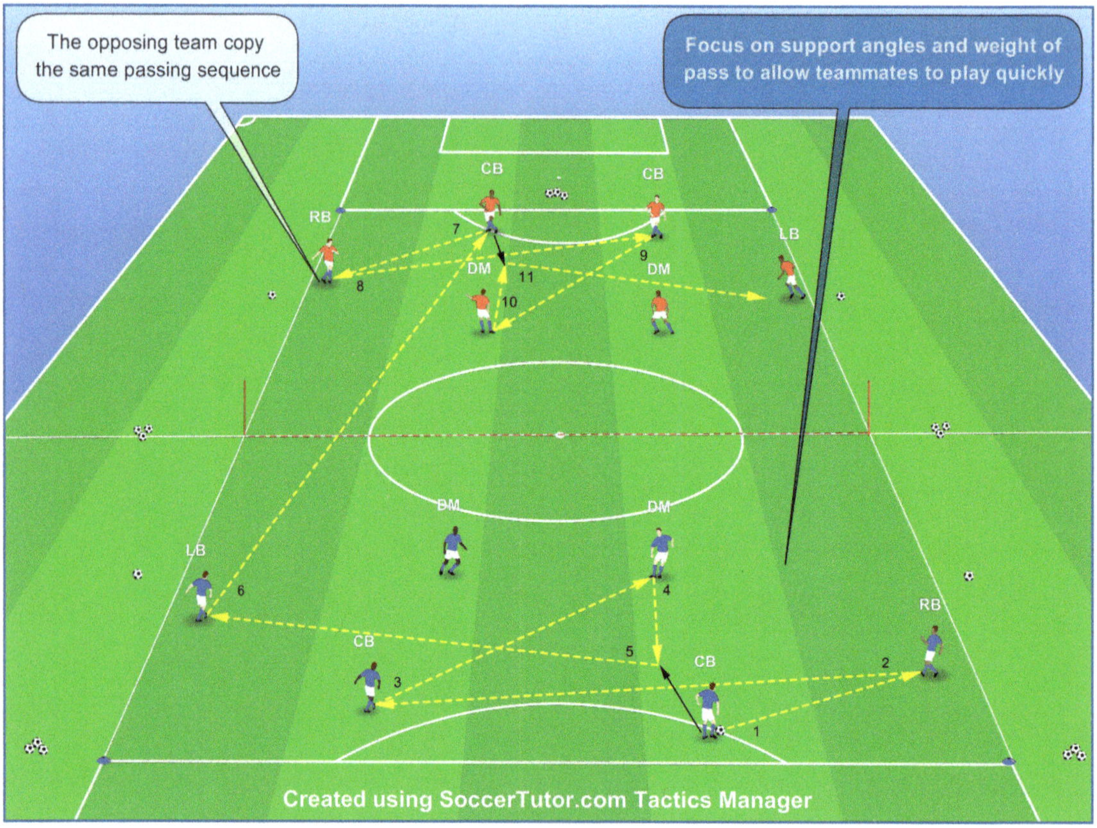

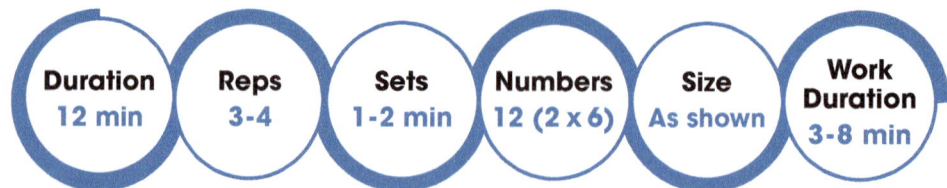

OBJECTIVE: Decision making, support angles, body shape, and passing range.

- Players are in 2 teams of 6. In this example, the 4-2-3-1 is used with the back 4 + 2 defensive midfielders, but you can adjust to different formations.
- One team starts (blues) with free decision making for a build up pattern before passing to the opposite team.
- The opposite red team must copy the same pattern before returning the ball.
- Change the team roles halfway through so both sets of players create and copy patterns an equal amount of time.
- **Progression:** Add a forward who plays with both teams.

Duration	Reps	Sets	Numbers	Size	Work Duration
12 min	3-4	1-2 min	12 (2 x 6)	As shown	3-8 min

Extensive Technical Practices (Large Spaces)

13. Positional and Rotational Combination Play Tactical Patterns

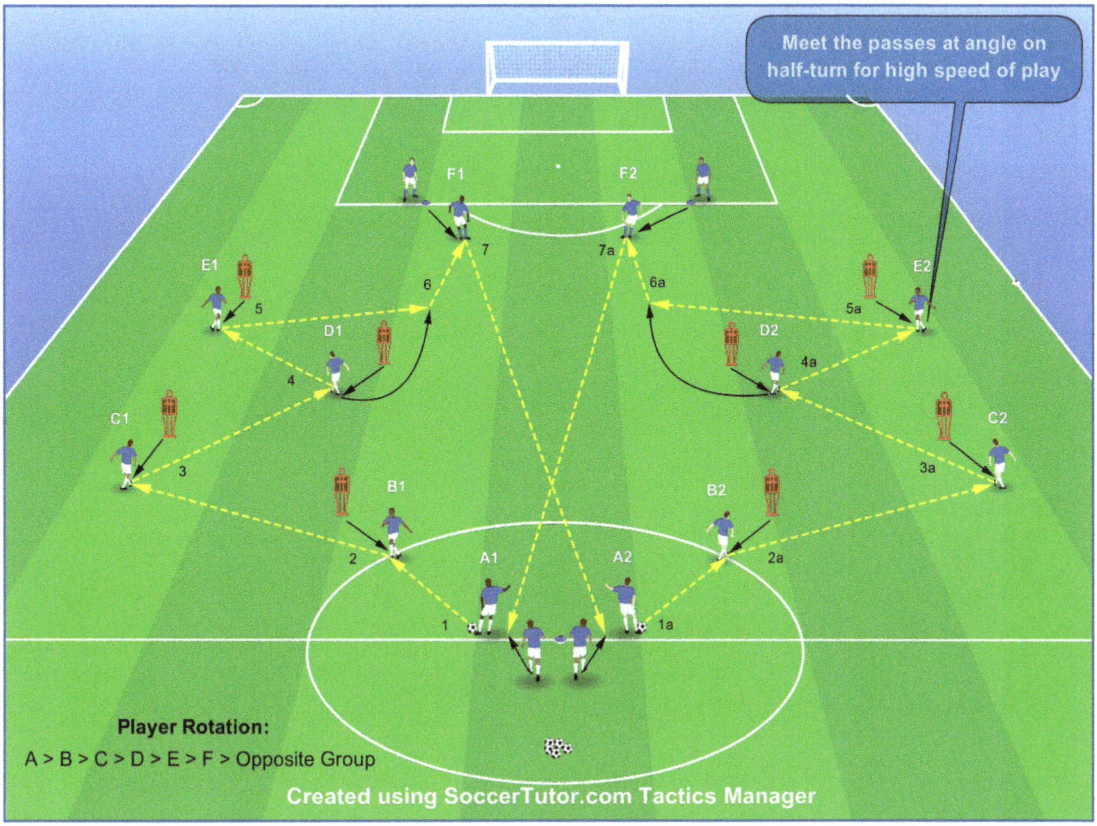

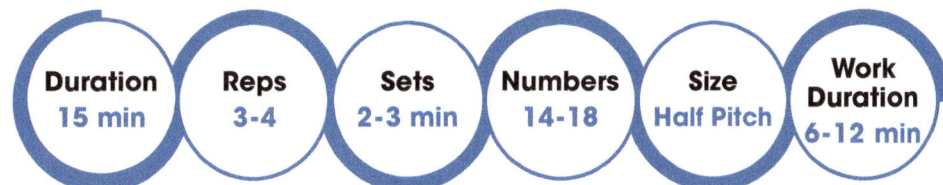

Duration	Reps	Sets	Numbers	Size	Work Duration
15 min	3-4	2-3 min	14-18	Half Pitch	6-12 min

OBJECTIVE: Forward passing, tactical combinations, and progressive passing patterns.

- Two balls start simultaneously from **A1** and **A2**.
- **A1/A2** pass to **B1/B2**, who play wide to **C1/C2**. **C1/C2** pass inside to **D1/D2**.
- **D1/D2** play a one-two with **E1/E2**, run around the mannequin to receive the return, and then pass to **F1/F2**.
- **F1/F2** pass to Position A1/A2 on the opposite side and the same sequence is repeated on both sides of the pitch.
- All players follow their passes and rotate positions through both sides.
- **Variation:** **C1/C2** pass **E1/E2**, who set the ball for **D1/D2** to pass to **F1/F2**.

Extensive Technical Practices (Large Spaces)

14. Positional and Rotational Combination Play Tactical Patterns with Switch of Play

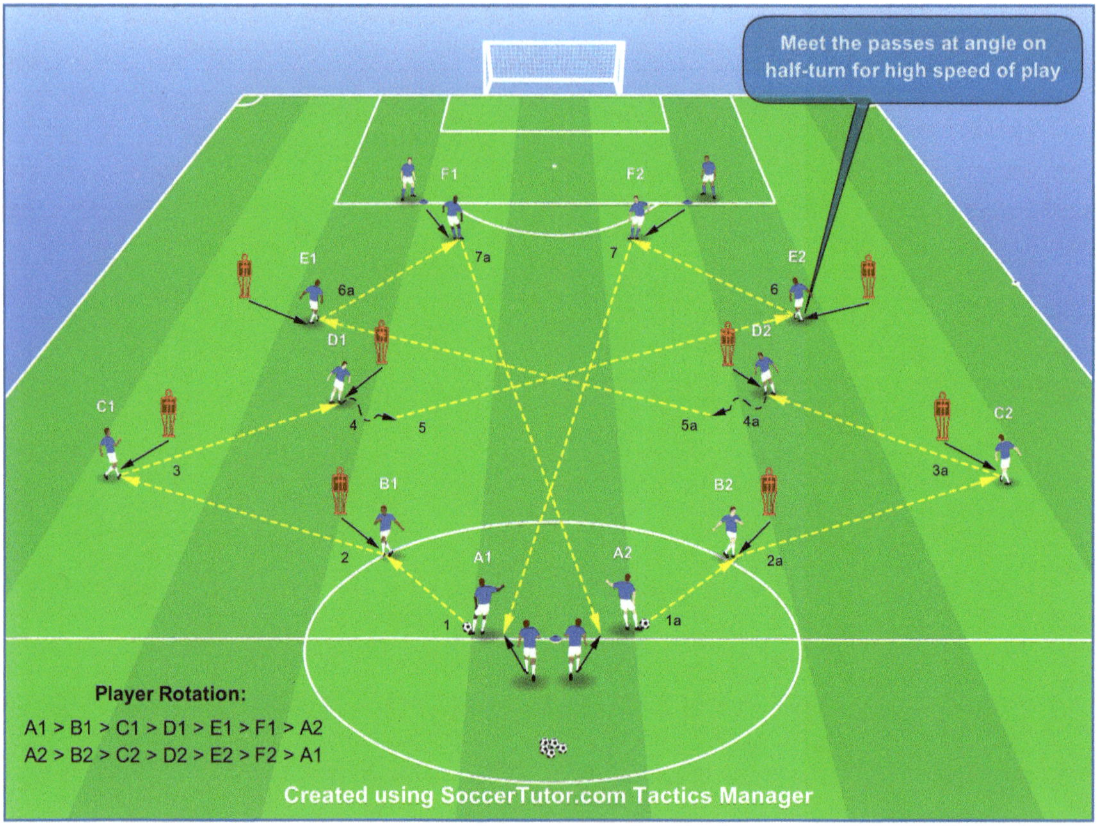

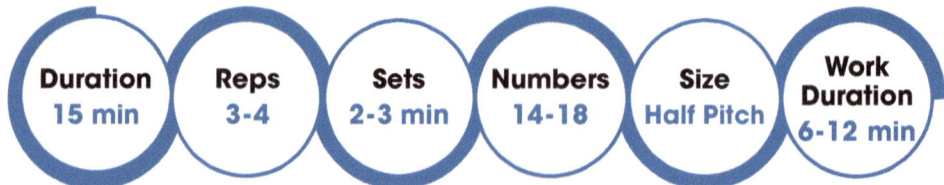

Duration	Reps	Sets	Numbers	Size	Work Duration
15 min	3-4	2-3 min	14-18	Half Pitch	6-12 min

OBJECTIVE: Switching play, tactical combinations, and progressive passing patterns.

- Two balls start simultaneously from **A1** and **A2**. **A1/A2** pass to **B1/B2**, who play wide to **C1/C2**. **C1/C2** pass to **D1/D2**.

- **D1** turns inside and switches the play to the opposite group with a pass to **E2**. **D2** does the same by passing to **E1**.

- **E1** passes to **F1**, who passes to the opposite side: Position A2. **E2** passes to **F2**, who passes to Position A1.

- Even though there is a switch of play to the opposite group, all players rotate in order on their side after their passes.

- The same sequence is repeated from the next players waiting at Positions A1/A2.

Extensive Technical Practices (Large Spaces)

15. Real Madrid Breaking Lines and Support Play Combinations (Variation 1)

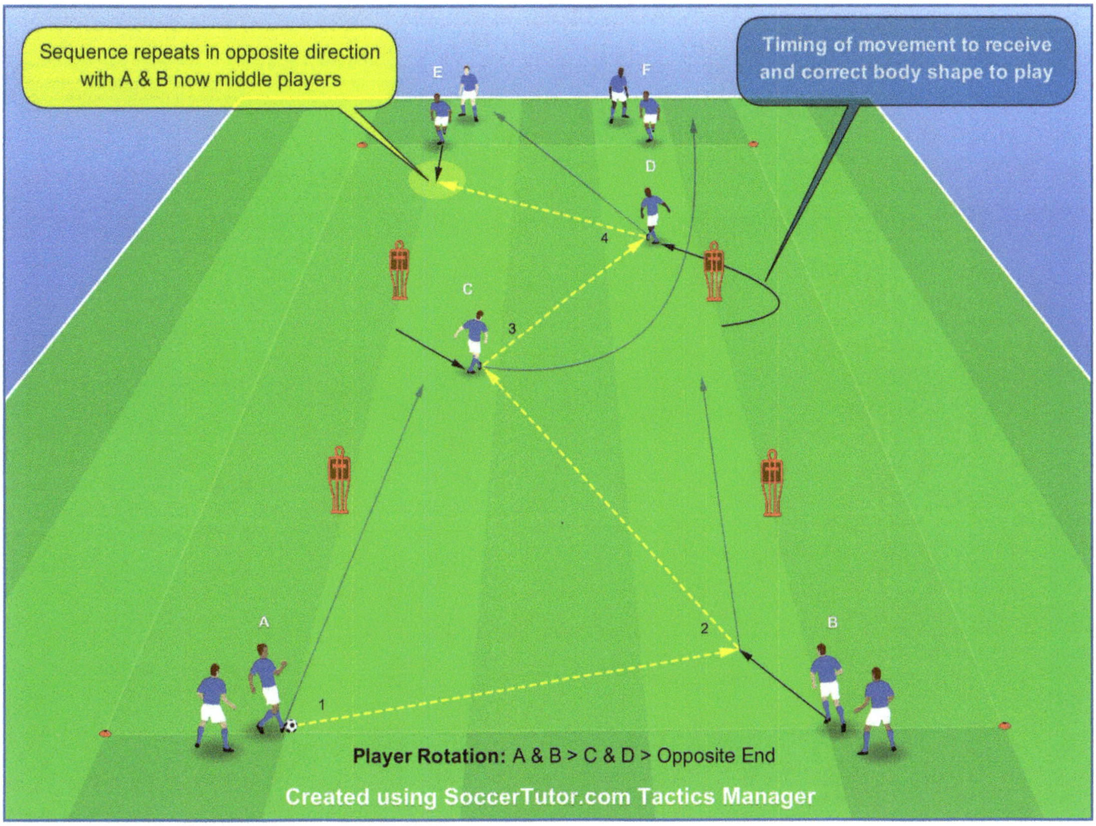

[Diagram: Players arranged in a 30x15 area. Callout "Sequence repeats in opposite direction with A & B now middle players". Callout "Timing of movement to receive and correct body shape to play". Players A, B at one end; C, D in middle with mannequins; E, F at opposite end. Numbered passing sequence 1-4. Player Rotation: A & B > C & D > Opposite End]

Duration	Reps	Sets	Numbers	Size (m)	Work Duration
15 min	3-4	2-3 min	10	30 x 15	6-12 min

OBJECTIVE: Play forward, breaking lines with attacking waves, and support play.

- The players are all in pairs. Two players are in the middle (**C** and **D**).
- **A** and **B** start. **A** passes across to **B**, who passes forward to **C**.
- **C** drop off to the mannequin to receive and then passes forward to **D**, who runs around the other mannequin to receive.
- **D** passes to **E**. **A/B** become the middle players and **C/D** move to the end. **E/F** repeat in the opposite direction.
- **Coaching Points:** Effective passing and receiving, with a focus on control and accuracy. Timing of movements to receive and correct body shape to play.

Extensive Technical Practices (Large Spaces)

16. Real Madrid Breaking Lines and Support Play Combinations (Variation 2)

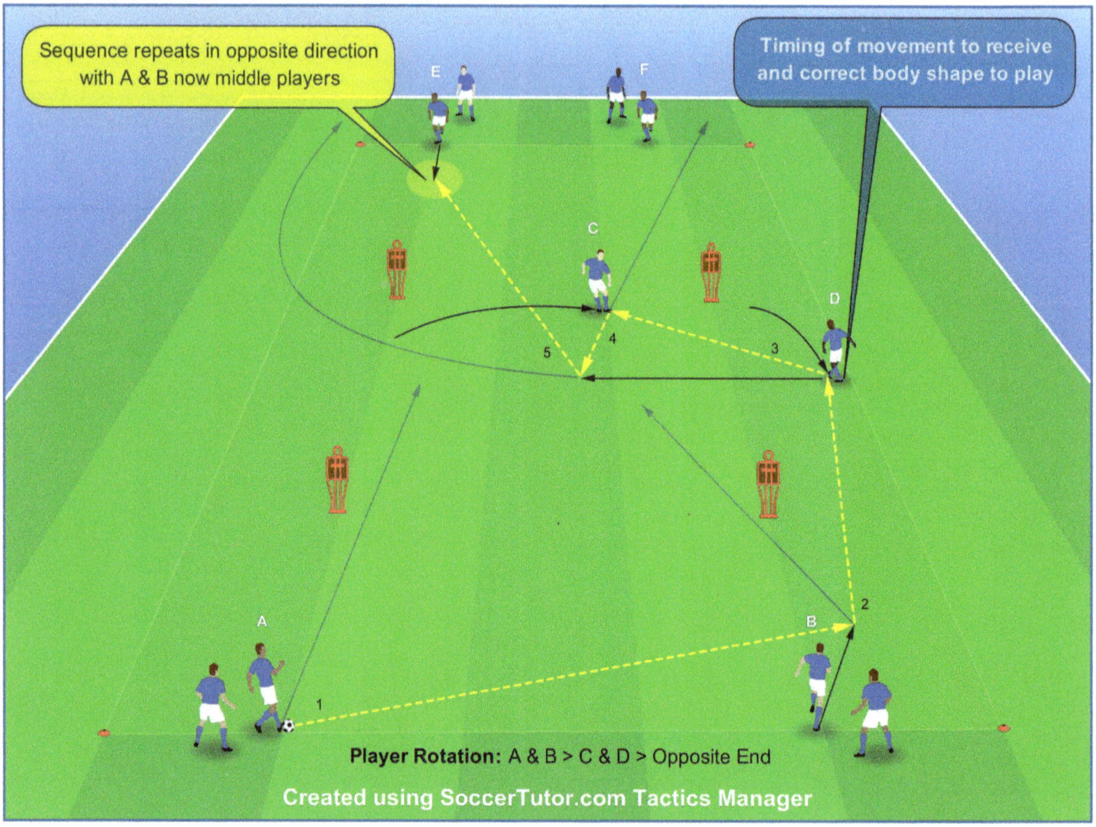

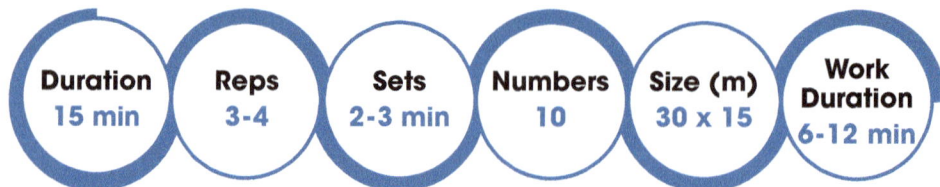

Duration	Reps	Sets	Numbers	Size (m)	Work Duration
15 min	3-4	2-3 min	10	30 x 15	6-12 min

OBJECTIVE: Play forward, breaking lines with attacking waves, and support play.

- This is a variation of the previous practice.
- This time, **D** moves wide to receive a vertical forward pass from **B**.
- From there, **D** plays a one-two with **C**, who shifts across to support, and then passes to **E**.
- **A/B** become the middle players and **C/D** move to the end. **E/F** repeat in the opposite direction.
- **Coaching Points:** Effective passing and receiving, with a focus on control and accuracy. Timing of movements to receive and correct body shape to play.

Extensive Technical Practices (Large Spaces)

17. Breaking Lines with Wide Combination Play Diamond Passing with Overlap

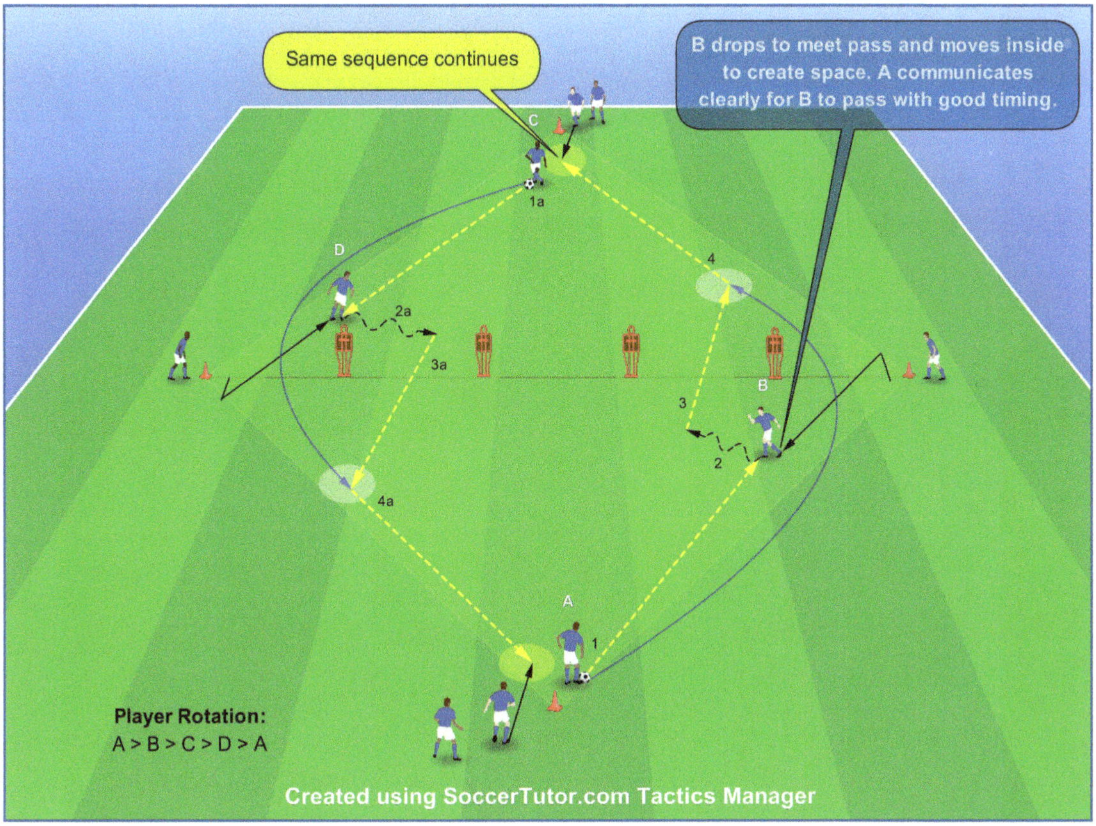

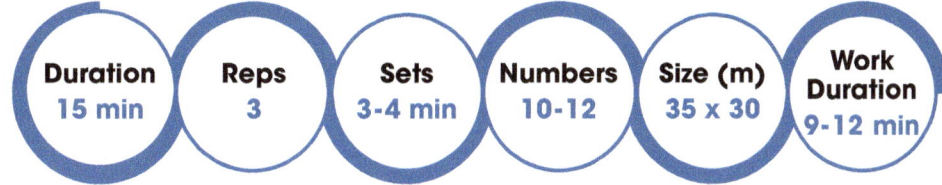

Duration	Reps	Sets	Numbers	Size (m)	Work Duration
15 min	3	3-4 min	10-12	35 x 30	9-12 min

OBJECTIVE: Forward passing, breaking lines, and wide combination play with overlap.

- Starting from the base of the diamond, the aim is to move the ball forward, breaking through the mannequin line.
- The circuit starts with 2 balls simultaneously from **A** and **C**.
- **A/C** pass to **B/D**, who makes a double movement (go long to come short), receive, and then deliver a through pass for the overlapping run of **A/C**.
- The sequence is completed with **A/C's** pass to the next player waiting at Position A/C, as the sequence repeats.
- **Progression:** Add passive defenders to apply pressure to the receivers (**B** & **D**).

Extensive Technical Practices (Large Spaces)

18. Breaking Lines with Wide Combination Play Diamond Passing with Underlap

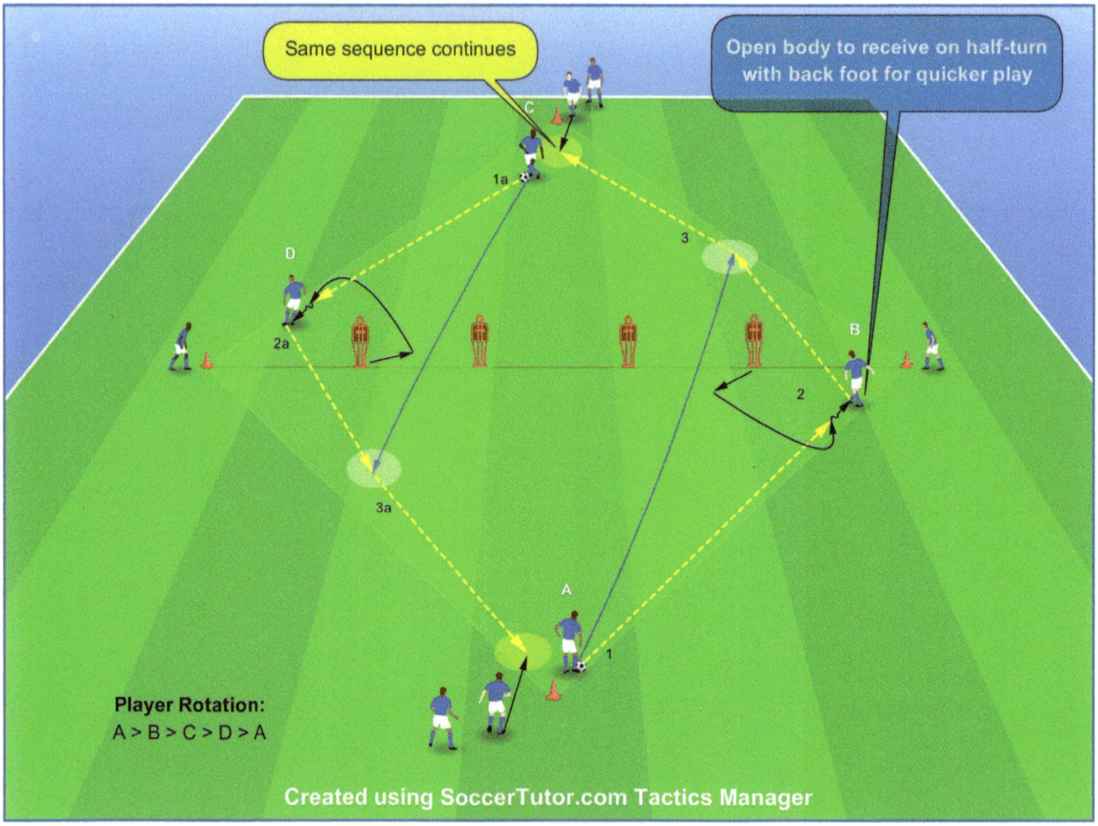

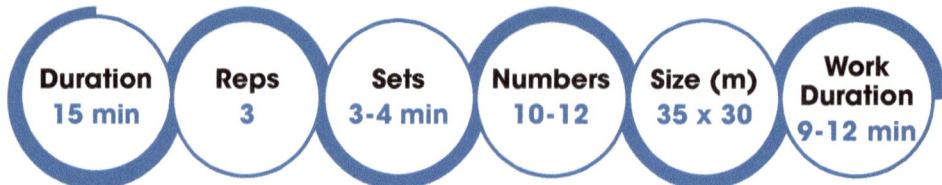

Duration	Reps	Sets	Numbers	Size (m)	Work Duration
15 min	3	3-4 min	10-12	35 x 30	9-12 min

OBJECTIVE: Forward passing, breaking lines, and wide combination play with underlap.

- This is a variation of the previous practice, now with an underlap run.
- **A/C** pass to **B/D**, who make a double movement to receive, and then deliver an outside pass for the inside underlap run of **A/C** to break the mannequin line.
- The sequence is completed with **A/C's** pass to the next player waiting at Position A/C, as the sequence repeats.
- **Progression:** Add passive defenders to apply pressure to the receivers (**B** & **D**).
- **Coaching Points:** Quality, accuracy, and weight of pass, good control, support angles/timing, and communication.

Extensive Technical Practices (Large Spaces)

19. Third Man Run Overlaps Passing Combinations with Defensive Pressure

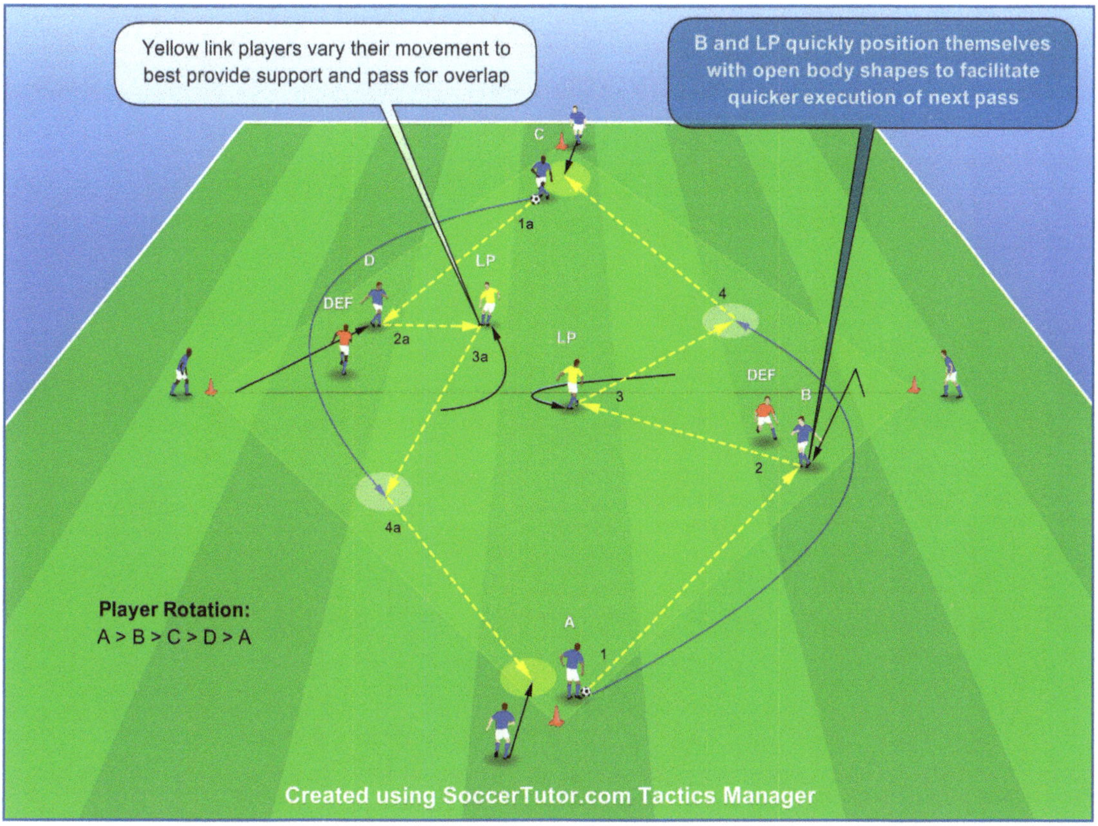

[Diagram: Yellow link players vary their movement to best provide support and pass for overlap. B and LP quickly position themselves with open body shapes to facilitate quicker execution of next pass. Player Rotation: A > B > C > D > A]

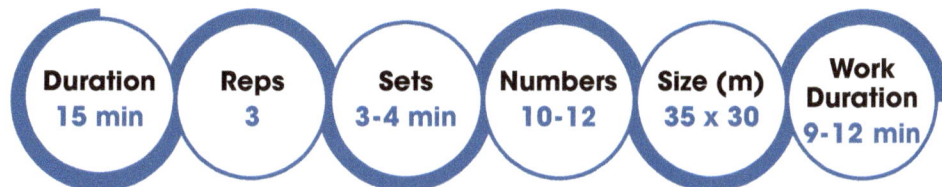

Duration	Reps	Sets	Numbers	Size (m)	Work Duration
15 min	3	3-4 min	10-12	35 x 30	9-12 min

OBJECTIVE: Forward passing, wide combination play passing, and breaking lines.

- This is a variation of the previous 2 practices. The 4 mannequins have been removed, replaced with 2 red defenders.
- There are also 2 link players (**LP**) who assist in the blue players' combinations.
- **A/C** pass to **B/D**, who make a double movement (go long to come short).
- **B/D** receive and pass inside to the link player (**LP**), who passes for the overlapping run of **A/C**.
- The sequence is completed with **A/C's** pass to the next player waiting at Position A/C, as the sequence repeats.

Technical to Maximise Performance

Extensive Technical Practices (Large Spaces)

20. Breaking Lines Passing Combination Waves in Pairs

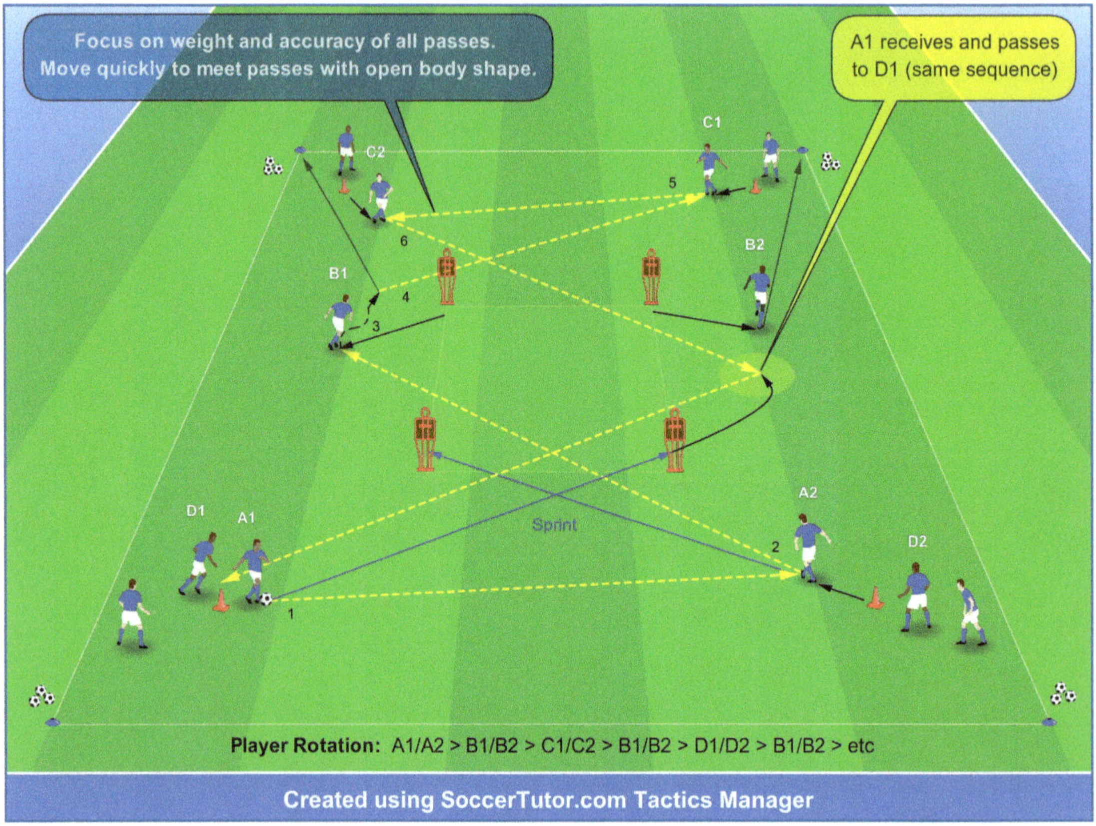

Focus on weight and accuracy of all passes. Move quickly to meet passes with open body shape.

A1 receives and passes to D1 (same sequence)

Player Rotation: A1/A2 > B1/B2 > C1/C2 > B1/B2 > D1/D2 > B1/B2 > etc

Created using SoccerTutor.com Tactics Manager

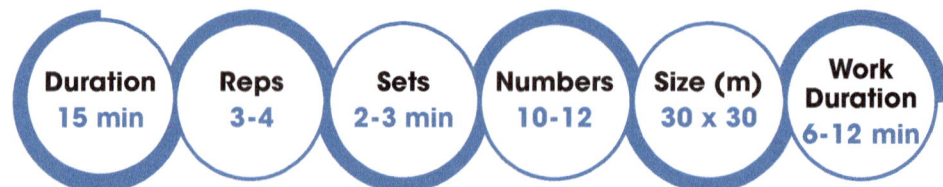

OBJECTIVE: Forward passing, progressive passing, switching play, and awareness.

- **B1** and **B2** start near the 2 top mannequins in the central square.
- **A1** passes to **A2**, who passes diagonally through the central square for the wide movement of **B1**, as shown.
- **B1** opens up, takes a good directional first touch, and passes diagonally to **C1**.
- **A1** and **A2** sprint to the bottom 2 mannequins. **B1** and **B2** move to Positions C1 and C2.
- **C1** passes to **C2**, who passes diagonally through the central square for the wide movement of the new **B1** (previously **A1**) and the same sequence continues.

Extensive Technical Practices (Large Spaces)

21. Rangers FC Breaking Lines with Forward Passing Circuit

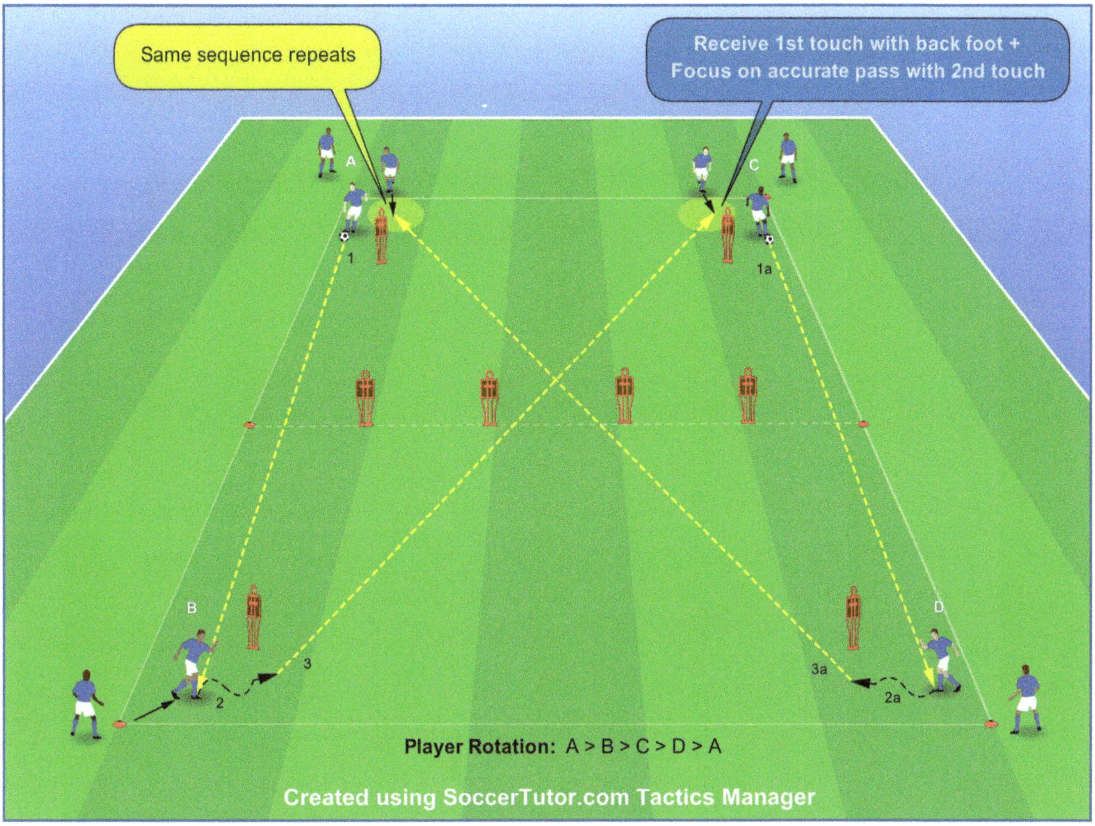

[Diagram: 40x30m area with mannequins forming an opposing line. Players A and C pass forward to B and D through gaps. Annotations: "Same sequence repeats" and "Receive 1st touch with back foot + Focus on accurate pass with 2nd touch". Player Rotation: A > B > C > D > A. Created using SoccerTutor.com Tactics Manager]

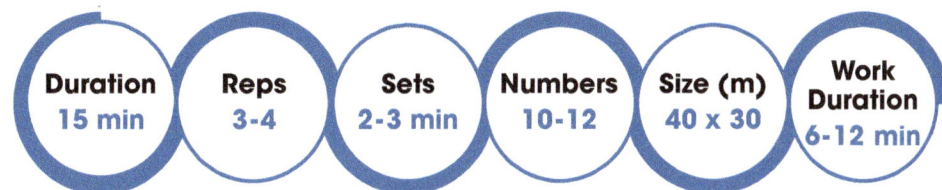

Duration	Reps	Sets	Numbers	Size (m)	Work Duration
15 min	3-4	2-3 min	10-12	40 x 30	6-12 min

OBJECTIVE: Technical passing, playing forwards, and breaking opposition lines.

- Within the 40 x 30 m area, position mannequins to form an opposing line so the players have to play through the gaps. There are 2 balls which start simultaneously from **A** and **C**.
- **A/C** pass forward to **B/D**, who open up to receive behind the mannequin.
- **B/D** take a good directional touch and play a firm ground diagonal pass to the next players waiting at Position A/C.
- **Coaching Points:** Focus on the players' ability to work the ball through available spaces, enhancing their awareness and precision in tight situations.

Extensive Technical Practices (Large Spaces)

22. Rangers FC Breaking Lines with Dribbling Circuit + Finish

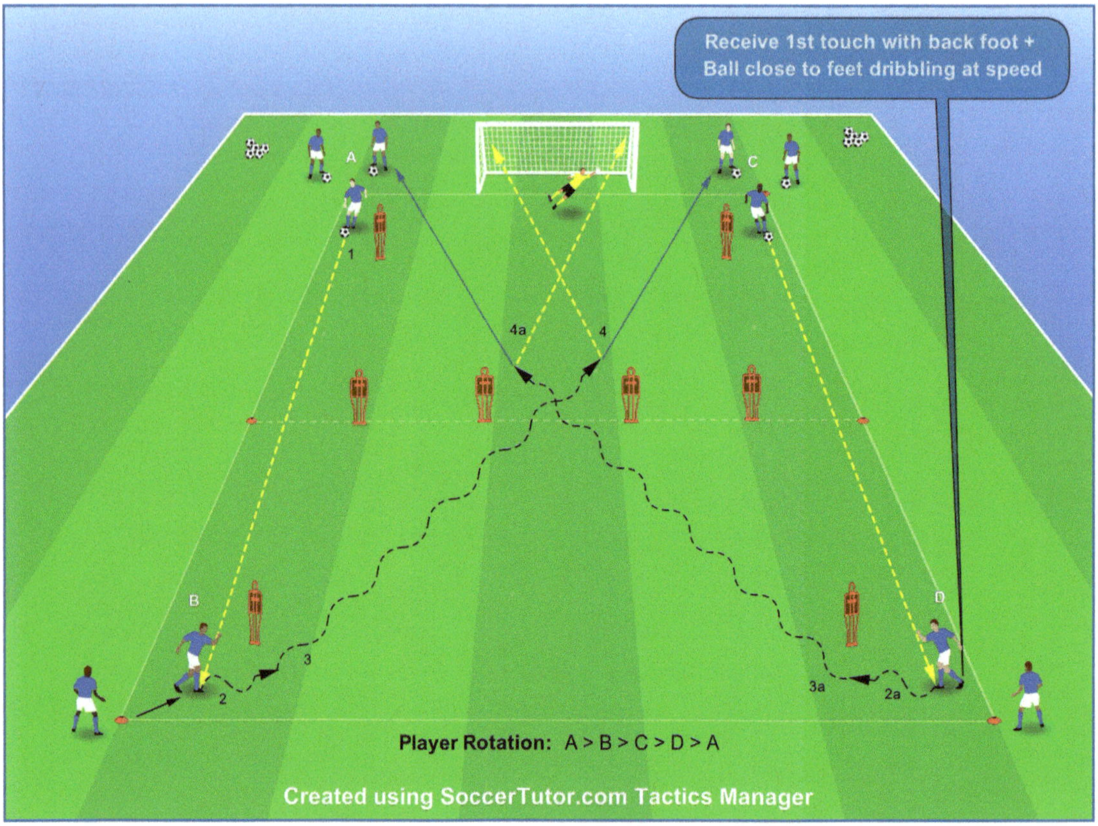

[Diagram: Receive 1st touch with back foot + Ball close to feet dribbling at speed. Player Rotation: A > B > C > D > A. Created using SoccerTutor.com Tactics Manager]

Duration	Reps	Sets	Numbers	Size (m)	Work Duration
15 min	3-4	2-3 min	10-12	40 x 30	6-12 min

OBJECTIVE: Technical passing, playing forward, breaking lines, dribbling, and finishing.

- In this progression of the previous practice, add a goal + GK at the top.
- **A/C** pass forward to **B/D**, who open up to receive behind the mannequin.
- **B/D** then drive with the ball to break the opposition's line (mannequins), and then shoot to try and score.
- As soon as the shot is taken, the next player waiting at <u>Positions A and C</u> can start the same sequence with a new ball.
- **Coaching Points:** Focus on the players' ability to work the ball through available spaces, enhancing their awareness and precision in tight situations.

Extensive Technical Practices (Large Spaces)

23. Two Way Forward Passing, Wide Combinations, and Finishing

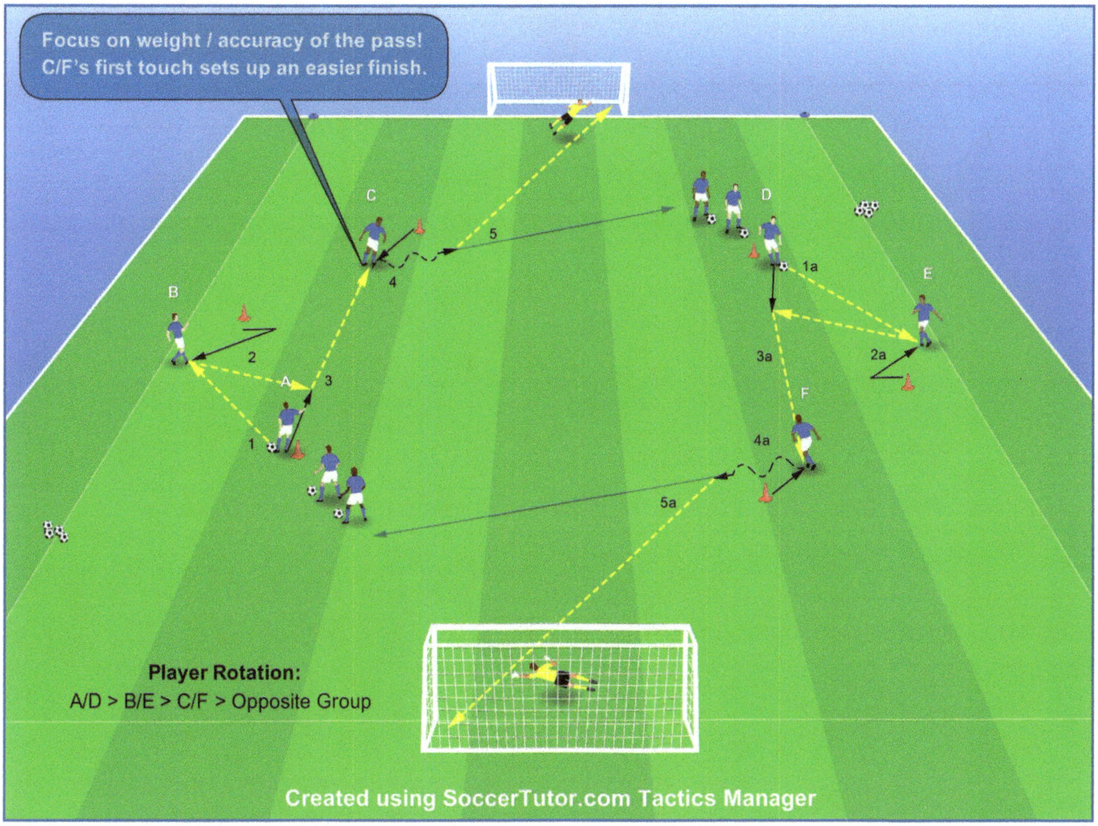

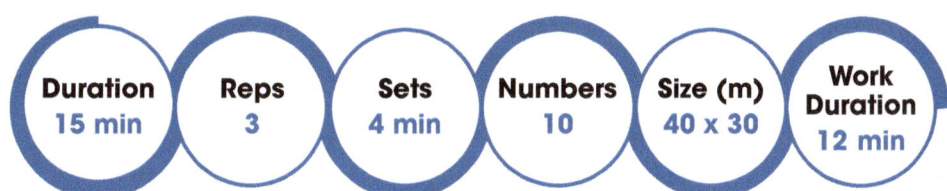

Focus on weight / accuracy of the pass! C/F's first touch sets up an easier finish.

Player Rotation:
A/D > B/E > C/F > Opposite Group

Duration	Reps	Sets	Numbers	Size (m)	Work Duration
15 min	3	4 min	10	40 x 30	12 min

OBJECTIVE: Forward passing, wide combination play passing, and finishing.

- Players work in groups of 10 and 2 balls start simultaneously with **A** and **D**.
- **A/D** pass to **B/E**, who set the ball back for **A/D** (one-two).
- **A/D** pass to **C/F**, who take a directional touch past the cone towards goal, and then try to score with a side foot finish.
- After shooting, **C/F** move to the opposite group.
- **Coaching Points:** Quality, accuracy, and weight of pass, good first touch/control, and support play. Communication, timing of movement, and focus on controlled and accurate finishing.

Extensive Technical Practices (Large Spaces)

24. Tactical Build Up to Break Lines and Finish Attacks (Various Patterns)

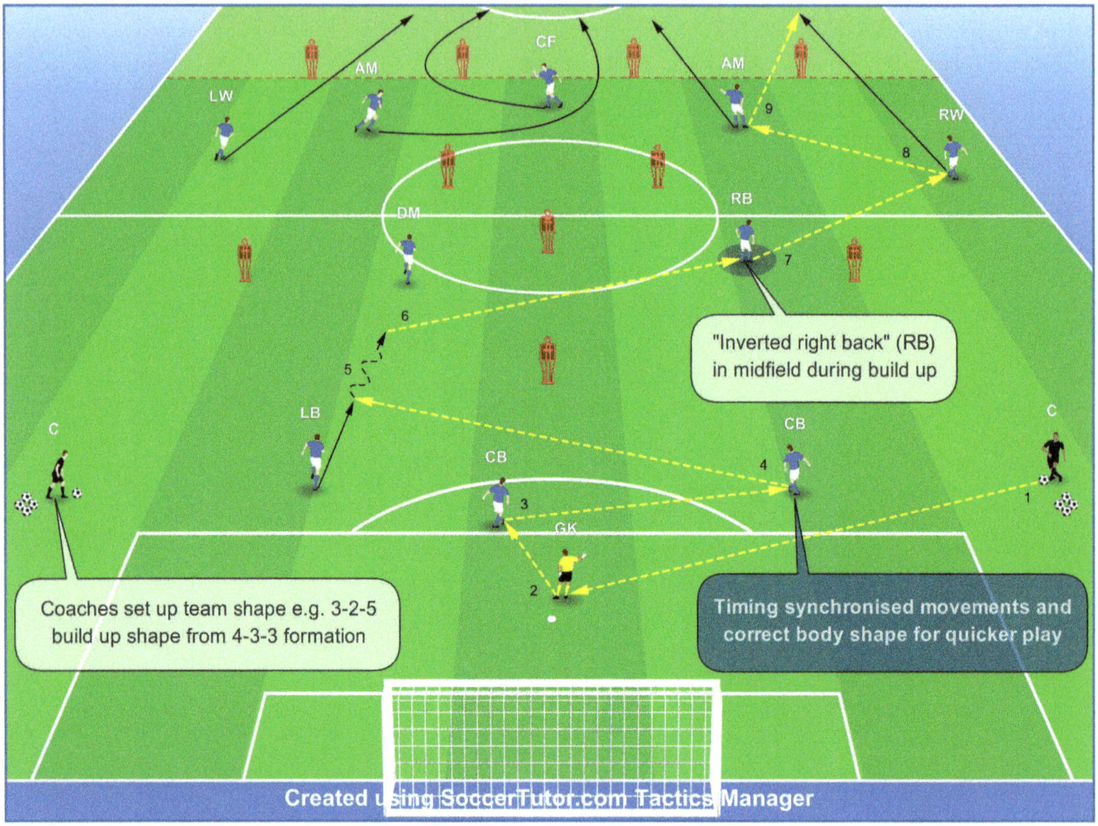

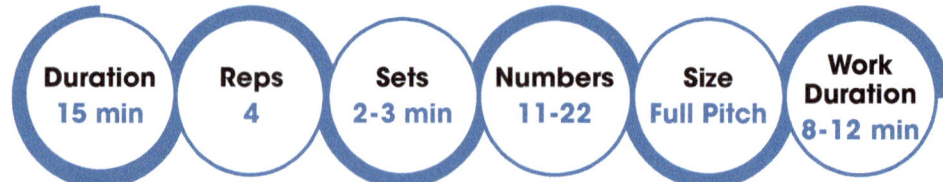

"Inverted right back" (RB) in midfield during build up

Coaches set up team shape e.g. 3-2-5 build up shape from 4-3-3 formation

Timing synchronised movements and correct body shape for quicker play

Duration	Reps	Sets	Numbers	Size	Work Duration
15 min	4	2-3 min	11-22	Full Pitch	8-12 min

OBJECTIVE: Tactical build up play, playing forward, breaking lines, through passes.

- Two coaches start on either side of the pitch and pass to the **GK** to start.
- The patterns are set by the coach and the diagram shows one example.
- Players move the ball around and through mannequins which represent the opposition's defensive shape.

- **Progressions:** Set a time limit from start to finish. All players must touch the ball. 4 players have to make runs into the box.
- **Coaching Points:** Movements and counter-movements to create space, passes in wide areas, and attacking runs to finish in the box.

ADVANCE YOUR CAREER.
BECOME A BETTER COACH...

Accredited & Endorsed Online Football Science & Performance Coaching Courses

The premier global online football education platform, accredited and endorsed by leading universities and elite clubs, which offers cutting-edge courses in football science and performance coaching. Trusted by the football community worldwide, it provides unparalleled expertise and knowledge to aspiring coaches and professionals alike.

 www.ISSPF.com / Email: contact@ISSPF.com

   @ISSPFed

ADAM OWEN PERFORMANCE CONSULTANCY

As an esteemed leader and educator in the field of technical and sporting development, performance coaching and football science, AO Performance maintains partnerships with elite football and sports organisations across Europe and beyond. Additionally, collaborations extend to grassroots sports clubs, universities, and FIFA member associations, spanning various levels of expertise. To explore potential collaborations for you or your organisation, reach out to learn more about opportunities now or in the future.

 www.aoperformance.co.uk / Email: contact@aoperformance.co.uk

@adamowen1980

References

- Casal, C.A., Maneiro, R., Ardá, A. and Losada, J.L., 2019. Gender differences in technical-tactical behaviour of La Liga Spanish football teams.

- Cordón-Carmona, A., Villavicencio Álvarez, V.E., Morales, S.C., Mon-López, D., García-Aliaga, A. and Refoyo, I., 2023. The influence of pass length and height in Europe's top 5 leagues in men's football. The Open Sports Sciences Journal, 16(1).

- Cordón-Carmona, A., García-Aliaga, A., Marquina, M., Calvo, J.L., Mon-López, D. and Refoyo Roman, I., 2020. What is the relevance in the passing action between the passer and the receiver in soccer? Study of elite soccer in La Liga. International Journal of Environmental Research and Public Health, 17(24), p.9396.

- Fernandez-Navarro, J., Ruiz-Ruiz, C., Zubillaga, A. and Fradua, L., 2020. Tactical variables related to gaining the ball in advanced zones of the soccer pitch: analysis of differences among elite teams and the effect of contextual variables. Frontiers in Psychology, 10, p.502088.

- González-Rodenas, J., Ferrandis, J., Moreno-Pérez, V., López-Del Campo, R., Resta, R. and Del Coso, J., 2023. Differences in playing style and technical performance according to the team ranking in the Spanish football La Liga. A thirteen seasons study. Plos one, 18(10), p.e0293095.

- Lago-Ballesteros, J.; Lago, C.; Rey, E. The effect of playing tactics and situational variables on achieving score-box possessions in a professional soccer team. J. Sports Sci. 2012, 30, 1455–1461.

- Zhou, C., Gómez, M.Á. and Lorenzo, A., 2020. The evolution of physical and technical performance parameters in the Chinese Soccer Super League. Biology of sport, 37(2), pp.139-145.

Free Trial

Football Coaching Specialists Since 2001

Tactics Manager
Create your own Practices, Tactics & Plan Sessions!

Tactics Manager App

SoccerTutor.com

Football Coaching Specialists Since 2001

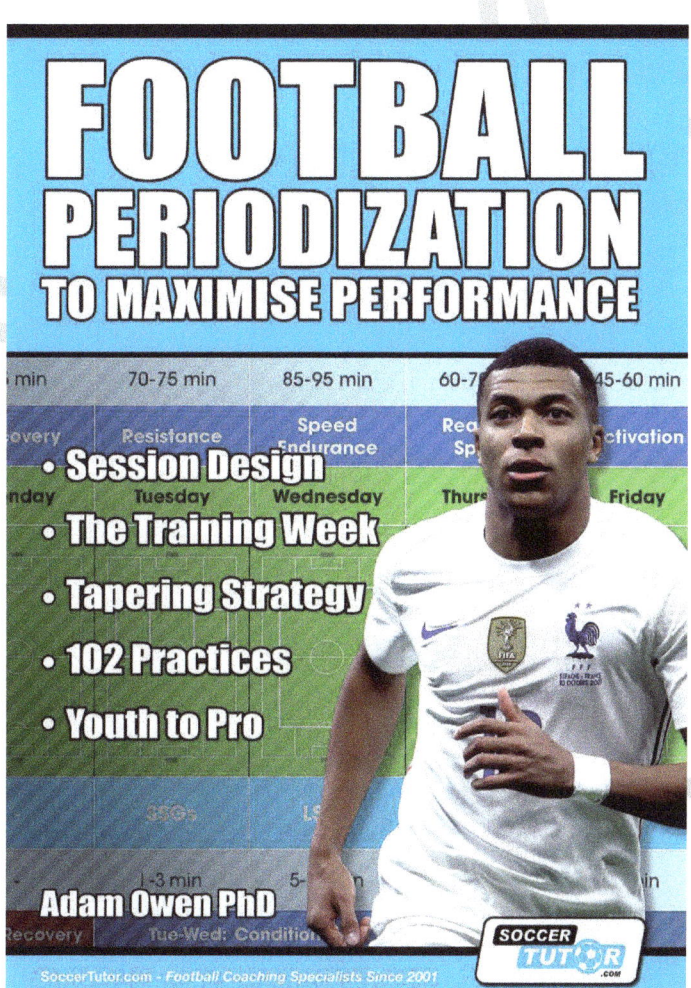

Coaching Books Available in Full Colour Print and eBook!
PC | Mac | iPhone | iPad | Android Phone / Tablet | Chromebook

FREE Coach Viewer **APP**

SoccerTutor.com

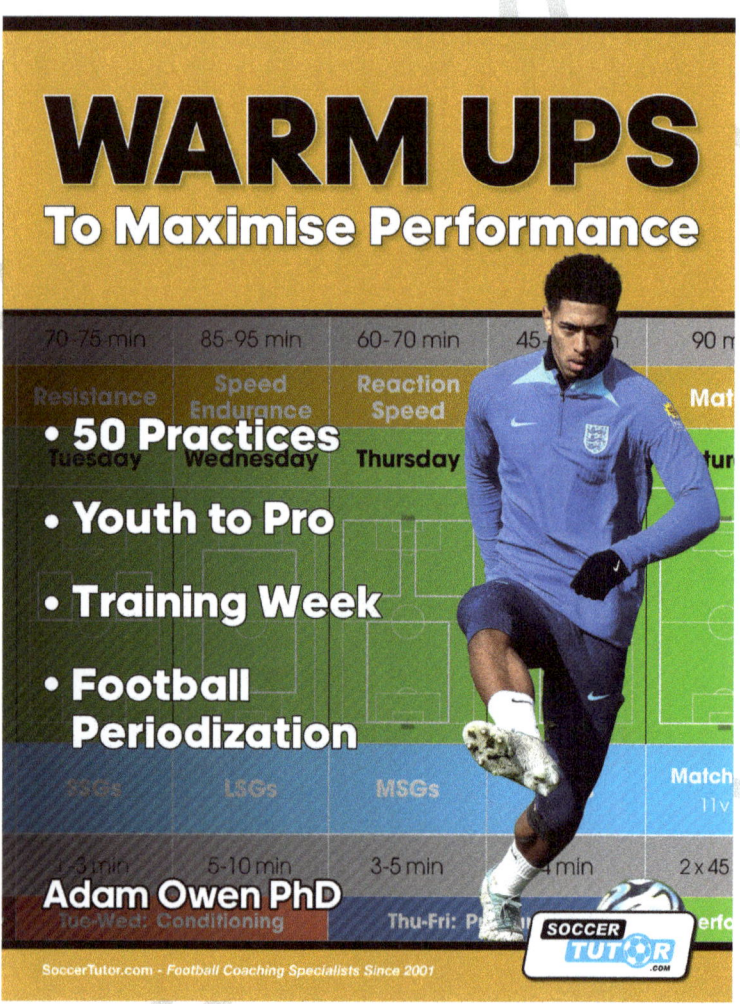

Football Coaching Specialists Since 2001

Coaching Books Available in Full Colour Print and eBook!
PC | Mac | iPhone | iPad | Android Phone / Tablet | Chromebook

FREE Coach Viewer **APP**

SoccerTutor.com

Football Coaching Specialists Since 2001

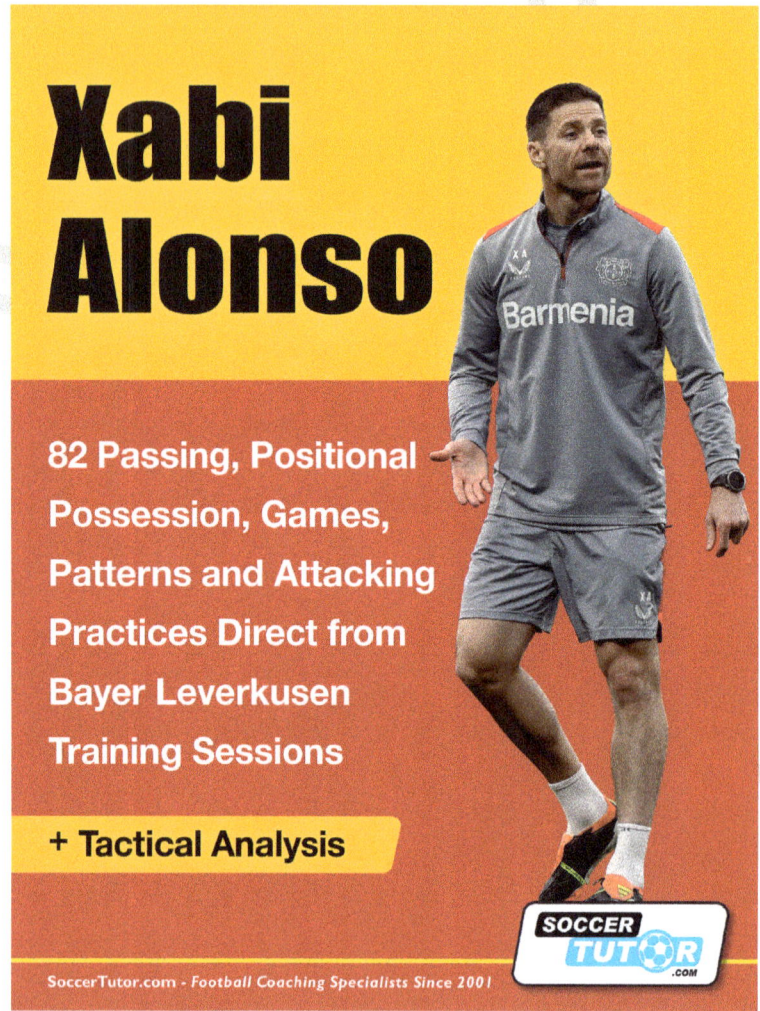

Coaching Books Available in Full Colour Print and eBook!
PC | Mac | iPhone | iPad | Android Phone / Tablet | Chromebook

 **FREE** Coach Viewer **APP**

SoccerTutor.com

Football Coaching Specialists Since 2001

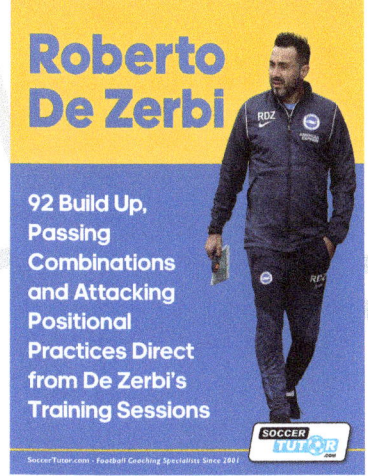

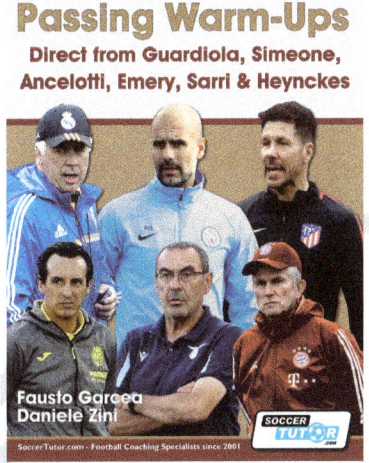

Coaching Books Available in Full Colour Print and eBook!
PC | Mac | iPhone | iPad | Android Phone / Tablet | Chromebook

 **FREE** Coach Viewer **APP**

SoccerTutor.com

www.ingramcontent.com/pod-product-compliance
Lightning Source LLC
Chambersburg PA
CBHW061210230426
43665CB00028B/2966